FAIRIES
IN VICTORIAN ART

FAIRIES
IN VICTORIAN ART

CHRISTOPHER WOOD

Antique Collectors' Club

First published 2000
© 2000 Christopher Wood
World copyright reserved

ISBN 1 85149 336 0

The right of Christopher Wood to be identified as author of this work has been asserted by him in accordance with the Copyright, Designs and Patents Act 1988

All rights reserved. No part of this publication may be reproduced, stored in a retrieval system, or transmitted in any form or by any means electronic, mechanical, or photocopying, recording or otherwise, without the prior permission of the publisher

British Library Cataloguing-in-Publication Data:
A catalogue record for this book is available from the British Library

Frontispiece: John Anster Fitzgerald, *'The Fairies' Barque'* (detail, see page 108)
Contents page: Ernest Howard Shephard (1879-1976), *'The Earth-Made House'*

Printed in England by the Antique Collectors' Club Ltd., Woodbridge, Suffolk IP12 1DS
on Consort Royal Satin paper supplied by the Donside Paper Company, Aberdeen, Scotland

Contents

	page		page
Introduction	8	CHAPTER TEN John Anster Fitzgerald	98
CHAPTER ONE Origins	18	CHAPTER ELEVEN Richard Doyle and Charles Altamont Doyle	114
CHAPTER TWO Fairy Literature	24	CHAPTER TWELVE Lesser Fairy Painters	124
CHAPTER THREE Fairy Theatre	42	CHAPTER THIRTEEN The Pre-Raphaelites and Fairies	142
CHAPTER FOUR Fairy Ballet	52	CHAPTER FOURTEEN Fairy Illustrators 1850–1900	152
CHAPTER FIVE Fairy Music	58	CHAPTER FIFTEEN Arthur Rackham RWS	162
CHAPTER SIX The Early Victorians	62	CHAPTER SIXTEEN Fairy Illustrators After 1900	172
CHAPTER SEVEN Robert Huskisson	70	Further Reading	186
CHAPTER EIGHT Richard Dadd	74	Plate List	186
CHAPTER NINE Joseph Noel Paton RSA	86	Index	190

For Rosie with love

Acknowledgements

As always, I could not have compiled the illustrations for this book without the help of my friends in the art world. Among the dealers, I am especially grateful to Chris Beetles, Rupert Maas, Peter Nahum, David Mason and Simon Edsor, and their gallery assistants, who have all been unfailingly helpful and generous both with transparencies and information. At Sotheby's, Henrietta Pattinson has once again been tireless in tracking down owners and seeking their permission.

Among collectors, my thanks go to Christopher Forbes, Christopher Gridley, and Andrew Lloyd-Webber. I am also grateful to all the museums and art galleries from whom I have borrowed transparencies, and to the Bridgeman Art Library.

Suzanne Bailey has typed the manuscript and, most important of all, did the picture research. My thanks to Peter Butler, the designer, and Diana Steel of the Antique Collectors' Club for her support and encouragement. Finally, yet another thank you to my friend and literary agent, Andrew Best, for his skill and tact in unravelling the mysteries of contracts.

CHRISTOPHER WOOD

INTRODUCTION

In an utilitarian age, of all other times, it is a matter of grave importance that fairy tales should be respected…A nation without fancy, without some great romance, never did, never can, never will, hold a place under the sun.

CHARLES DICKENS
'HOUSEHOLD WORDS', VOL. 8, 1 OCTOBER, 1853

John Simmons, 'A Midsummer Night's Dream: Hermia and the Fairies' (1861). *One of the chief attractions of fairy painting for the mid-Victorians was that it made possible highly realistic and erotic pictures of female nudes. This was the type of fairy picture in which Simmons specialised.*

The Victorians desperately wanted to believe in fairies, because they represented one of the ways they could escape the intolerable reality of living in an unromantic, materialistic and scientific age. We tend to think of the Victorians as stern and moralistic, staring grimly out at us from early photographs, in their black top hats and frock coats. But Dickens was right in his perception that underneath that deceptively utilitarian surface, the Victorians yearned for 'some great romance'. In their art, their literature and their architecture, they were arch-romantics and dreamers, the true heirs of the Romantic Movement. In art, they gave us Pre-Raphaelitism, the greatest and most long-lasting romantic movement in English art. They also gave us some of the most extraordinary fairy paintings ever produced in any country at any time. Their contribution to the literature of fairy stories was also immense; it was the Victorians who gave us 'Alice's Adventures in Wonderland' and 'Peter Pan'. No one could say that the Victorians were 'a nation without fancy'.

Fascination with fairies and the fairy world was therefore just another facet of Victorian romanticism, part of the Victorian need for history, romance and

INTRODUCTION

Left: Edmund Dulac (1906).
'E was an exquisite Elf
Who enjoyed being quite by
   herself
She delighted to play
In an elegant way
With things she found on a
   shelf'.

Far left: John Anster Fitzgerald, 'The Intruders'. *The fairies' relationships with the animal kingdom was one of the recurring themes of Victorian fairy painting. Here fairies confront and tease a frog underneath a toadstool. Two fairies wield a thorn branch, as if it were a wand to change the frog. Fitzgerald's pictures often combine humour and cruelty in a way he perceived characteristic of the fairy world.*

fantasy. It found expression in most of their art forms – not only in painting but also in illustration, literature, poetry, theatre, ballet and music. In painting, the golden age of fairy painting lasted from about 1840 to 1870, but it can be traced back well before this, to the work of Blake and Fuseli in the late eighteenth century. Fairies lived on after 1870, mainly in the world of children's books and their illustrations. This is a tradition that survives today, in the work of many modern illustrators whose work still echoes both the subject matter and the style of their Victorian predecessors.

What makes Victorian fairy paintings unique is that Victorian painters, for the first time, attempted to combine fairy painting with 'truth to nature'. Under the influence of Ruskin and the Pre-Raphaelite Brotherhood, they tried to paint fairies realistically and accurately, with the greatest possible attention to detail. Such a combination of reality and fantasy may seem an impossibility, yet the Victorians attempted it, and this is what gives their fairy paintings their

INTRODUCTION

strange, and at times, disturbing intensity. What I want to do above all in this book is to look at fairy paintings as paintings, as one of the chapters in the story of Victorian art, and not just as documents. For that reason I think it important to illustrate details of many of the pictures, for it is in the detail that much of the fascination lies.

Like so much in Victorian art, fairy painting had a strong literary background. Fairies and folklore have a long literary history, going back to Shakespeare, Spenser and Milton, even to Chaucer. For the Victorians, it was books by two foreign writers that fuelled the craze for fairy stories, 'Grimm's Fairy Tales', first published in 1824, and later Hans Christian Andersen's 'Fairy Tales', published in the 1840s. The stories of the Brothers Grimm were illustrated by one of Dickens' finest illustrators, George Cruikshank (1792–1878), and this contributed greatly to their popularity. But by far the most fruitful source for fairy paintings were Shakespeare's two plays, 'A Midsummer Night's Dream' and

John Anster Fitzgerald, 'In Fairyland'. *Walking by a stream with her pail, a milkmaid seems to have strayed unwittingly into fairyland. It was country people like the milkmaid who frequently reported seeing fairies, especially in woods, hills and by streams. Fitzgerald was the most inventive and the most dedicated of Victorian fairy painters.*

INTRODUCTION

'The Tempest', which were to inspire many of the greatest fairy paintings, by Dadd, Paton, Millais, Huskisson and others. Indeed, almost all fairy paintings before 1850 were inspired by Shakespeare, the majority of them by 'A Midsummer Night's Dream'. Only after 1850 did Victorian fairy painting develop a style of its own, independent of literary allusion, particularly in the work of John Anster Fitzgerald, the greatest and most prolific of the fairy painters. But the connections between fairy painting and fairy literature were always strong, as I hope to demonstrate. To understand fairy painting, it is essential to understand its literary dimension.

Another important source of imagery was the emerging romantic movement in ballet. One of its main themes was the supernatural, in which a spirit forms a relationship with a mortal. This was the theme of 'La Sylphide', pioneered in London by the famous ballerina Marie Taglioni. Its success spawned a series of

William Edward Frost, 'Fairy Lovers'. *For a human to fall in love with a beautiful fairy was always dangerous, and usually had unhappy consequences. It represented an unattainable ideal, perfect love, but in the end was an illusion. Frost (1810–77), and his mentor William Etty, both influenced those fairy painters who specialised in female nudes, such as Robert Huskisson and John Simmons.*

INTRODUCTION

Right: Arthur Rackham, 'The Daisy Fairy'. *Country people have always associated fairies with flowers. Victorian painters and illustrators frequently depict fairies playing among flowers, plants, and undergrowth, as Rackham, greatest of the Edwardian illustrators, has done here.*

Far right above: 'Frances and the Fairies', *one of the Cottingley fairy photographs. In 1917 two Yorkshire girls claimed to have seen fairies near the village of Cottingley, and produced photographs to support their assertions. The episode generated huge public interest and heated debate. Sir Arthur Conan Doyle, a firm believer in the possibility of a fairy world, wrote a book defending the girls, 'The Coming of the Fairies' (1922).*

Far right below: Arthur Rackham, 'Decorative Border with Fairies and Birds'.

similar ballets, populated by nymphs, sylphs, dryads, wilis, peris, naiads, and undines, all of whom were to make further appearances in Victorian fairy paintings. In the 1850s, Charles Kean, a leading actor-manager of the day, mounted lavish productions of 'A Midsummer Night's Dream' and 'The Tempest', both with elaborate technical stage effects. There are clearly strong links between the Victorian theatre and fairy painting, particularly ballet and ballet music, all subjects I shall explore in more detail.

Much has been made of the Victorian obsession with spiritualism, spirit-rapping, and the unseen world. The Society for Psychical Research was founded in 1882. 'Tea and table-turning' became a fashionable craze in the late Victorian period and famous mediums of the day became international celebrities. Spirit photography was also popular, and led to the celebrated 'Cottingley fairies' dispute. The connection between all this and fairy painting is not entirely clear, but it undoubtedly helped to create an atmosphere in which fairy painting and literature could flourish. Between artist and public there was a zone of common ground, in which both sides were prepared to believe. There can be no doubt that the fascination with the supernatural went hand-in-hand with the Victorian crisis of faith. Religious doubt seemed to drive the Victorians to take refuge ever deeper in the worlds of fantasy and the imagination. As the painter Burne-Jones put it, 'the more materialistic science becomes, the more angels I shall paint'.

Belief in fairies and folklore was also seen by the Victorians as part of the disappearing customs of country life. 'Village tradition,' wrote Thomas Hardy, 'a vast amount of unwritten folklore, local chronicle, local topography and nomenclature, is absolutely sinking, has nearly sunk, into eternal oblivion'. To counter this, the Folklore Society was founded in 1878. Belief in fairies still survived in Victorian times in most country districts, especially in the Celtic fringe – the West Country, Wales, Scotland and Ireland. The Victorians somehow hoped that the 'little people' were still there, but had gone into hiding. With the exception of the Scottish painter Noel Paton, and Daniel Maclise, who was Irish, none of the other

INTRODUCTION

Far right: John Anster Fitzgerald, 'Ariel'.

*Fairy folks
Are in old Oaks*

Trees have always been associated with fairies and spirits. Like all fairies, this tree fairy is also close to the bird world. Victorian fairy paintings and illustrations frequently show fairies and birds together.

Below: Sir George Frampton, 'Peter Pan'. *A small bronze version of Frampton's celebrated Peter Pan statue of 1908, which still stands in Kensington Gardens, where many of the episodes of 'Peter Pan' were set.*

Victorian fairy painters was an expert on folklore.

Victorian painters of fairies fall into two main types – those who made a speciality of it, and those who only made occasional forays into the fairy world. Turner, Landseer and Millais only painted one fairy subject each. Noel Paton, the Scottish Pre-Raphaelite, painted only a small number of fairy subjects, but they are among the masterpieces of the genre. Even Richard Dadd, the most notorious of all the fairy painters, painted only about ten fairy pictures. Two Irish artists also contributed a few pictures to the fairy vogue – Francis Danby and Daniel Maclise.

The three specialists in fairies were Robert Huskisson, Richard Doyle and John Anster Fitzgerald. Their styles, subject matter and approach are all quite different, but the most interesting of the three is Fitzgerald. His pictures explore the world of dreams and nightmares in a uniquely individual way. More than any of the other Victorian fairy painters, Fitzgerald opens a window on the Victorian subconscious to reveal its dark secrets. The fascination of Fitzgerald's pictures, and of all Victorian fairy paintings, is that they offered the artist a way to explore those taboo subjects – sex, nudity, violence, even drugs – beneath the respectable cloak of art.

Fairy painting could hardly be described as a movement in itself. For most artists it was purely an occasional choice of subject, before moving on to other things. It is a tributary of Victorian art, rather than part of the mainstream. But it is a particularly fascinating tributary, and produced enough material to justify a book. It has already provided one very successful exhibition, at the Royal Academy in 1998.

After 1870, the vogue for fairy painting began to decline, but made an occasional appearance in the paintings of Atkinson Grimshaw, Edward Robert Hughes and others. In the world of children's books, however, fairies lived on, enjoying a new wave of popularity, thanks to the wonderful illustrations of Arthur Rackham, Edmund Dulac and many others. This was the golden age of the childrens' book, but a very different world from that of Dadd and Fitzgerald. It revolved much more around children; 'Peter Pan' was first performed in 1904, and has remained hugely popular to this day. The Victorian world is often thought to have come to an end in 1901, yet Estella Canziani's *The Piper of Dreams* (page 184), a fairy picture that dates from 1914, was hugely popular as a nursery print for many years after, and even found its way into the trenches in the First World War. The fairies, in truth, are always with us, to be interpreted in different ways by every generation, including our own. This book, I hope, will help us to understand what fairies meant to the Victorians.

CHAPTER ONE

ORIGINS

Far right: Circle of Francis Danby, 'Fairies by a Rocky Stream'. *Fairies in folklore are frequently associated with water; naiads and nixies are beautiful water sprites who lure men to their deaths in rivers and lakes. In Scotland a kelpie is a water spirit in the form of a water horse.*

There are fairies at the bottom of our garden
ROSE FYLEMAN
'FAIRIES AND CHIMNEYS', 1918

Although fairy literature has a long history in England, going back to Chaucer, the painting of fairy subjects only began in the late eighteenth century. One of its first practitioners was the poet and visionary, William Blake (1757–1827). Blake claimed to have seen fairies in his own garden:

I was walking alone in my garden, there was a great stillness among the branches and flowers, and more than common sweetness in the air; I heard low and pleasant sound, and I know not whence it came. At last I saw the broad leaf of a flower move, and underneath I saw a procession of creatures the size and colour of green and grey grasshoppers, bearing a body laid out on a rose-leaf, which they buried with songs and disappeared. It was a fairy funeral.

Blake produced a number of watercolours on fairy themes, including one of *Oberon, Titania and Puck with Fairies dancing* (overleaf), and others of Puck, or Robin Goodfellow, as he is traditionally known, getting up to mischief.

Both Sir Joshua Reynolds (1723–92) and Henry Fuseli (1721–1825) also turned to Shakespeare's 'A Midsummer Night's Dream' for their ventures into fairy pictures. They were among the artists commissioned by Alderman Boydell, a

ORIGINS

William Blake 'Oberon, Titania and Puck with Fairies dancing' (circa 1785). *Blake was a mystic and a poet, who believed implicitly in the spirit world and in fairies, who he thought of as rulers of the vegetable world. Here he depicts the reconciliation between Oberon and Titania, on the left, as a rural idyll, with fairies dancing in a ring, and Puck providing accompaniment on the castanets.*

successful city merchant, for a gallery of pictures based on subjects from Shakespeare. Begun in 1789, it eventually included nearly 150 pictures which were later all engraved, the resulting volume becoming known as 'Boydell's Gallery'.

Reynolds' contribution was an impish figure of *Puck*, seated on a toadstool, the ancestor of many a later Victorian Puck. Fuseli, who was deeply interested in folklore and the occult, chose two scenes involving Titania – *Titania and Bottom* (overleaf) and *Titania's Awakening*. In both pictures, Fuseli allowed his taste for the erotic and the macabre full rein, introducing a cast of fearsome characters from folk legend – a hooded night hag with a changeling, a fairy courtesan, witches, ghouls galore, one galloping on a mad horse, recalling Fuseli's famous and haunting picture *The Nightmare*. Fuseli was said to eat a plate of raw beef before going to bed to improve the quality of his dreams.

After Reynolds and Fuseli, fairy painting seems to have dropped out of fashion, although it features occasionally in the work of lesser artists, such as Henry Singleton (1766–1839) and Henry Howard (1769–1847). The visionary artist John Martin (1789–1854) was not exactly a fairy painter, but his biblical epics undoubtedly influenced the fairy painters, in particular his illustrations to Milton's 'Paradise Lost' (1827).

Francis Danby, 'Scene from A Midsummer Night's Dream' (1832) *One of the earliest of many Victorian depictions of the quarrel between Oberon and Titania. The Indian boy, the source of the quarrel, sleeps under a mushroom. A fairy hangs from an oxlip to light his taper from a passing glow worm.*

ORIGINS

Johann Heinrich Fuseli, 'Titania and Bottom' and detail (circa 1788–90). *Fuseli depicts Titania at the height of her infatuation with Bottom, changed into an ass. Typically, he has introduced threatening and grotesque elements in fairyland. To the left a hooded night hag clutches a changeling baby; on the right a fairy courtesan leads one of her victims, a bearded old man, on a leash. This is fairyland full of menace and danger.*

CHAPTER TWO

FAIRY LITERATURE

*You spotted snakes with double tongue,
Thorny hedgehogs, be not seen.
Newts and blindworms, do no wrong,
Come not near our Fairy Queen.*

WILLIAM SHAKESPEARE
'A MIDSUMMER NIGHT'S DREAM', ACT 2

Fairies have a long history in English literature, and the Victorians were the heirs to a rich literary tradition. Even by the age of Chaucer, the fourteenth century, fairies were seen as elusive beings who already belonged to a distant past. As the Wife of Bath explained in 'The Canterbury Tales':

Far right: Mary L. Gow, 'Fairy Tales' (1880). *By the 1880s the emphasis on fairy painting had shifted towards children, and children's books. This resulted in many charming pictures of Victorian children reading, though few so delightful as this one. Mary Gow (1851–1929) was the sister of a painter, Andrew Carrick Gow, and married to another painter, Sydney Prior Hall. She has ended up better-known than either of them.*

In th'olde dayes of Kyng Arthour…
Al was this land fulfild of fayerye.
The elf-queene, with hir joly compaignye
Daunced full oft in many a grene mede.
This was the olde opinion, as I rede;
I speke of manye hundred yeres ago.
But now kan no man se none elves mo…

Fairies were seen as part of an older race, like the Celts, who had fled westwards, taken to the hills, or simply disappeared. Europe also had a rich tradition of fairy literature, such as the medieval French prose romances. 'Huon of Bordeaux', a fifteenth century romance, marks the first appearance of Oberon, King of the Fairies. Oberon's name derives from Alberic, the dwarf of German legend, but

FAIRY LITERATURE

Right: John George Naish, 'Titania'. *Titania asleep afforded many a Victorian artist the opportunity to paint beautiful naked girls, either sleeping or fluttering about. Titania is here shown asleep in a rose bush, surrounded by beautiful and nubile attendants. Naish (1824–1905) was a figurative, landscape and marine painter who turned to fairy subjects in the 1840s and 1850s. His style owes much to the example of Etty and Frost.*

Far right: Stephen Reid, 'A Midsummer Night's Dream' (1907). *Inscribed with the famous fairies' admonition from Act 2. It is a common factor in all folklore that for animals or humans to disturb fairies, whether sleeping or engaged in fairy ceremonies, is always dangerous, and likely to arouse the fairies' anger.*

Shakespeare is known to have used 'Huon of Bordeaux' as a source for 'A Midsummer Night's Dream'. Titania's name probably came from Ovid's 'Metamorphoses', well known to Shakespeare, where she is a goddess descended from the Titans. In the 1570s, Spenser began to publish his long poem 'The Faerie Queene', with its famous opening line:

A gentle knight was pricking on the plaine.

The knight sets out on his adventures in the service of 'that greatest Glorious Queene of Faery lond'. The story is a chivalric quest, and was to provide many Pre-Raphaelite painters with subjects, but not fairy painters. They turned to Shakespeare.

FAIRY LITERATURE

In 'A Midsummer Night's Dream'(1595) and 'The Tempest' (circa 1611) Shakespeare made great use of fairy literature and traditional English folklore. A knowledge of both plays is helpful in understanding Victorian fairy paintings, for nearly all fairy pictures up to about 1850 were inspired by one or other play. References to both, therefore, crop up continuously in this book.

By far the greatest number of Victorian fairy paintings are based on 'A Midsummer Night's Dream'. This seems, above all others, to be the play that appealed to the imagination of painters. The characters who feature most often

are Oberon, Titania, Puck and Bottom. The fairies in the play, Peaseblossom, Cobweb, Moth and Mustardseed, rarely appear individually, but are depicted as Titania's attendants, carrying out her orders. They are the traditional 'little people', able to creep into acorn cups, and in danger of being drowned if a bee's honey bag breaks. Their job is to 'serve the Fairy Queen':

> I must go seek some dewdrops here,
> And hang a pearl in every cowslip's ear.

The most important of the fairies is Puck, or Robin Goodfellow, a traditional figure of mischief in English folklore, who causes upsets and accidents, but also helps the housewife about the home. Puck's role in 'The Dream' is as the servant of Oberon, whose bidding he carries out faithfully, though he cannot resist at times exceeding his orders. His main job is to squeeze the 'magic juice' into lovers' eyes when they are asleep, so that they then wake up and fall in love with the first person they see. Thus Titania wakes up and falls in love with Bottom the Weaver, one of the 'rude mechanicals', who has just been turned in to an ass. The main theme of the play is love, its confusions, its contradictions, and above all, its comic side. The course of love is explored through the adventures of four couples – Theseus, Duke of Athens, and Hippolyta, Queen of the Amazons, who are betrothed; Hermia and Lysander; Helena and Demetrius; and Oberon and Titania.

The quarrel between Oberon and Titania sets the whole action of the play in motion. Oberon demands that Titania hands over to him 'a little changeling boy, To be my henchman,' and Titania refuses. The implication is that their quarrel unleashes the malevolent forces of nature, spreads dissension and misunderstanding, and causes storms and tempest. For the fairies are close to nature, indeed they are part of nature, and understand its ways. Thus Oberon's famous speech:

> I know a bank where the wild thyme blows,
> Where oxslips and the nodding violet grows,
> Quite over-canopied with luscious woodbine,
> With sweet musk-roses, and with eglantine;
> There sleeps Titania some time of the night,
> Lull'd in these flowers with dances and delight;
> And there the snake throws her enamell'd skin,
> Weed wide enough to wrap a fairy in.

Many painters used quotations from this beautiful passage as titles for their fairy painting. Most would have seen Charles Kean's production of 'A Midsummer

Night's Dream' in 1856, in which the eight-year-old Ellen Terry played Puck.

Traditionally, when fairies are disturbed, angry or quarrel amongst themselves, this generally brings bad luck and misfortune to mortals. As Shakespeare's contemporary John Lyly wrote in 'The Fairy Reproach':

> Pinch him, pinch him, black and blue,
> Saucie mortals must not view
> What the Queen of Stars is doing,
> Nor pry in to our fairy wooing.

Shakespeare sets his fairy scenes in a wood at night, for this is when reason sleeps, and dreams and nightmares take over. The play is in essence about the power of the mind, or the imagination, over love; Oberon and Titania and the fairies

John Anster Fitzgerald, 'The Land of Nod'. *Fitzgerald was one of the first Victorian fairy painters to explore the connection between fairies and dreams. This lady seems undisturbed by the fairies hovering about her chair; in the room beyond other fairies seem to be taking fairy tea. In some pictures, however, Fitzgerald conjured up much more nightmarish dreams than this (see Chapter Ten).*

FAIRY LITERATURE

Circle of Sir Joseph Noel Paton, 'Dreams in Fairyland'. *Surprisingly, it is naked fairies that feature in the dreams of this Victorian lady.*

represent the irrational, the inexplicable and the comic side of love. Dawn brings back the sun and a new day, and all the discords and confusions of the night dissolve. Harmony is restored, Oberon, Titania and the fairies may cause disharmony and confusion, but in the end their influence is seen as benevolent.

'The Tempest' also inspired many fairy paintings, though nothing like as many as 'The Dream'. It is an enigmatic and mysterious play, and therefore not easy to depict in visual terms. The whole play has a dream-like quality, unlike 'The Dream' which alternates between reality and fantasy. The most important character is the magician and wizard Prospero, who manipulates all the characters like puppets. His familiar, or spirit helper, is the sprite Ariel who, unlike Puck, is a purely ethereal creature, longing to escape from Prospero back to the ether where he belongs. The character of Ariel is the one, above all, that appealed to Victorian painters. Most popular of all was Ariel's first song:

> Come unto these yellow sands,
> And then take hands.
> Curtsied when you have and kissed
> The wild waves whist,
> Foot it featly here and there;
> And, sweet sprites, the burden bear.

In most pictures, Ariel is depicted as part of a group of nymphs and sea sprites, dancing and disporting on a rocky coast. The other common depiction of Ariel is as a single figure, singing his famous song before being set free:

> Where the bee sucks, there suck I,
> In a cowslip's bell I lie;
> There I couch when owls do cry.
> On the bat's back I do fly
> After summer merrily.
> Merrily, merrily shall I live now,
> Under the blossom that hangs on the bough.

Most Victorian painters would have seen one of the many celebrated productions of 'The Tempest', such as William Macready's of 1838, or that by Charles Kean in 1857. Both productions made use of elaborate stage effects among which Ariel was able to fly through the air supported by moving wires. Priscilla Horton created a sensation as Ariel in Macready's play of 1838, and was painted in the role by Daniel Maclise (page 46). However, apart from Ariel, 'The Tempest', offered no opportunities for the fairy painter.

After the death of Shakespeare, fairy literature continued to flourish throughout the seventeenth and eighteenth centuries. 'The History of Tom Thumb, His Life and Death' first appeared in 1630, and has remained a popular story to this day. In Victorian times a dwarf calling himself General Tom Thumb became a huge attraction at the Egyptian Hall on London's Piccadilly. The painter Benjamin Robert Haydon, who had an exhibition of his work in the Egyptian Hall at the same time, watched in despair as the crowds queued up to look at

FAIRY LITERATURE

Right: Richard Doyle, 'The God Thor drives the Dwarfs out of Scandinavia, by throwing his hammer at them' (1878). *The Brothers Grimm and Hans Christian Andersen popularised German and Danish mythology in England. The Victorians also explored Nordic mythology – William Morris, in particular, was obsessed by the subject and devoted many years to writing his versions of the Icelandic sagas.*

General Tom Thumb and took no notice of his paintings.

In the 1620s Ben Jonson wrote a poem entitled 'Robin Goodfellow':

> From Oberon, in fairyland,
> The king of ghosts and shadows there,
> Mad Robin, I at his command.
> Am sent to view the night-sports here.

Robert Herrick also wrote a series of fairy poems, featuring Oberon and Queen Mab. One, 'Oberon's Feast' (1648) could well describe a Victorian fairy picture by Richard Doyle:

> A little mushroom table spread,
> After short prayers, they set on bread;
> A Moon-parcht grain of purest wheat,
> With some small glit'ring gritt, to eate
> His choyce bitts with; then in a tree
> They make a feast lesse great than nice.

Milton also refers to Queen Mab and fairies in 'L'Allegro' (1632), and in 'Paradise Lost' (1667) he compares the fallen angels to 'Faerie Elves', following a popular belief that the fallen angels fell short of Hell and became fairies. Alexander Pope in 'The Rape of the Lock' (1714) refers to fairies as winged beings, their wings an iridescent rainbow of colours. Pope's imagery conjures up Victorian fairy paintings:

> Some to the Sun their insect-Wings unfold,
> Waft on the Breeze, or sink in Clouds of Gold...
> Loose to the wind their airy Garments flew,
> Thin glitt'ring Textures of the filmy Dew;
> Dipt in the richest Tincture of the Skies,
> Where light disports in ever-mingling Dies,
> While ev'ry Beam new transient Colours flings,
> Colours that change whene'er they wave their Wings.

In the eighteenth century, many of the most popular fairy tales came from France, including 'The Arabian Nights', which gave us the stories of 'Puss in Boots', 'Cinderella', 'Beauty and the Beast' and 'The Sleeping Beauty'. All of these became popular as illustrated children's books and pantomimes in Victorian times. The story of 'The Sleeping Beauty' was retold by the French writer Charles Perrault in his 'Histoires' or 'Tales of Mother Goose', and it was from this source that Burne-Jones took the theme for his great cycle of four pictures, *The Briar*

FAIRY LITERATURE

Rose. One English writer to gather together old ballads and folk-tales in the eighteenth century was Bishop Thomas Percy (1729–1811), whose 'Reliques of Ancient English Poetry' was published in 1765. This became a source for many later writers, in particular Sir Walter Scott.

By the Victorian period, Nordic mythology was becoming popular, and both William Morris and Burne-Jones became interested in it while at Oxford in the

FAIRY LITERATURE

John Tenniel, 'A Fairy Piper'. *Sir John Tenniel (1820–1914) worked as a cartoonist on 'Punch' for most of his life, but he illustrated many books as well, most famously both Lewis Carroll's masterpieces, 'Alice's Adventures in Wonderland' and 'Through the Looking Glass'.*

1850s. Icelandic sagas became one of Morris' great passions, and he translated 'Sigurd the Volsung' in 1876, the same year that Wagner's 'Ring Cycle' was performed at Bayreuth. The Pre-Raphaelites were also great admirers of the romantic poets, particularly Coleridge, Shelley and Keats, all of whom wrote some fairy poetry. Coleridge wrote 'The Song of the Pixies' in 1793, and Shelley wrote an early poem about Queen Mab. Keats' 'La Belle Dame Sans Merci' (1819), although not a fairy story, tells of a fairy being who casts a powerful spell over men. This was to become one of the most popular of all subjects for Victorian romantic painters, from J.W. Waterhouse through to Frank Dicksee and Frank Cadogan Cowper.

In the nineteenth century, many English scholars and antiquarians were becoming interested in mythology and fairy lore, and publishing large tomes on the subject. One was Thomas Keightley's 'The Fairy Mythology' (1828), while another popular Victorian work was J.G. Frazier's 'The Golden Bough' (1890). Such scholars were characterised as rather boring pedants by George Meredith in 'The Ordeal of Richard Feverel' and by George Eliot in 'Middlemarch', where Dr. Casaubon devotes his life to researching a 'Key to all the Mythologies' which is never published. One important compilation of British folk tales was S.C. Hall's 'Book of British Ballads' (1842–44). Hall hoped to do for English folk and fairy tales what the Brothers Grimm had done for the German. Many of the illustrations were by fairy artists, including Richard Dadd, John Tenniel, John Gilbert, Noel Paton, E.H. Corbould, William Bell Scott, and Alfred Crowquill. Hall also produced 'Midsummer Eve – a Fairy Tale of Love' in 1848, with illustrations by many of the same artists, and several by Robert Huskisson. In 1878 the Folklore Society was founded; it continues to research the subject to this day.

A writer who published a great deal on fairy mythology was Walter Scott. Not only a novelist and a poet, Scott was a passionate collector of folk tales and fairy legends, many of which still survived in Scotland as folk ballads. These he published in 1801–2 as 'Minstrelsy of the Scottish Border'. This was followed by 'The Lay of the Last Minstrel' (1805) and 'The Lady of the Lake' (1810), both of which contain fairy ballads, for instance 'Alice Brand' which describes a 'Fairy Rade':

> 'Tis merry, 'tis merry in Fairy-land,
> When fairy birds are singing,
> When the court doth ride by their monarch's side,
> With bit and bridle ringing.

These poems brought Scott fame and fortune, and also carried Scottish folklore to a wider audience. They remained hugely popular throughout the Victorian period and inspired many Victorian painters. Queen Victoria was an avid fan of 'The Lady of the Lake' which also inspired Noel Paton's *The Fairy Raid* of 1867, one of the greatest fairy pictures (see pages 91–95).

Scott corresponded with and encouraged other writers in the field, in particular the Scottish writer James Hogg (1770–1835) known as the Ettrick Shepherd, whose ballads inspired many Scottish painters. Scott also knew of the work of two Irish antiquaries, Thomas Crofton Croker (1798–1854) author of 'Fairy Legends and Traditions of the South of Ireland', and Thomas Keightley (1789–1872) another scholar in the same field. It was Croker who influenced the young Daniel Maclise in his early years in Cork, while Maclise provided some of the illustrations for Croker's book.

More importantly, Scott corresponded with the Brothers Grimm in Germany, who sent him a copy of their 'Kinder und Hausmärchen' of 1812. These were translated into English by Edgar Taylor in 1823 and 1826. They were an instant success, and remained popular for the rest of the nineteenth century. Hans Christian Andersen's 'Fairy Tales' were not published until the 1840s, and they and Grimm's stories became the most popular of all Victorian children's books, endlessly re-published, and illustrated by many different artists. The success of Grimm's tales was also largely due to the remarkably imaginative illustrations of George Cruikshank, who went on to illustrate several of Dickens' early novels. Cruikshank later became a fanatical crusader for temperance, and his 'Fairy Library' of 1853 retells the stories of 'Hop o' my Thumb' and 'Cinderella' as temperance tracts. Dickens criticised Cruikshank for this, writing that 'it is a matter of grave importance that Fairy tales should be respected'. Although he wrote very few fairy

Joseph Noel Paton, 'Titania Asleep'.

FAIRY LITERATURE

George Cruikshank, Jnr., 'A Fairy Dance.' *Dancing has always played a part in fairy folklore and fairy painting:*

By the moone we sport and play,
With the night begins our day;
As we daunce, the deaw doth fall.
　　Anonymous English poem

tales, Dickens passionately believed in them, and thought that they had nurtured his imagination as a young man. Both Ruskin and Thackeray each wrote a fairy tale, although Thackeray's 'The Rose and the Ring' (1855) was something of a spoof:

　　Fairy roses, fairy rings,
　　Turn out sometimes troublesome things.

Ireland has always had a particularly rich fairy literature, and fairy folklore is still very much alive in country districts. One Irish poet who made something of a speciality of fairies was William Allingham (1824–89), husband of the watercolourist Helen Allingham (1848–1926). It was his collection of poems entitled 'The Music Master', published in 1855, that contained Rossetti's illustration *The Maids of Elfen Mere*. This was seen and greatly admired by Burne-Jones and William Morris in Oxford, and they both determined to go to London and meet Rossetti, whose pupils they later became. Burne-Jones' first illustrations, done while he was at Oxford, were for a book entitled 'The Fairy Family'. He later suppressed them, but all eighty-eight illustrations survive and have been published in a modern edition (see page 144). They owe much to German illustration, and to the work of George Cruikshank in particular. Both Millais and Arthur Hughes also contributed illustrations to 'The Music Master'.

It was Allingham's poem 'The Fairies', published in 'Day and Night Songs' (1860) that opened with the classic lines:

> Up the airy mountain,
> Down the rushy glen,
> We dare not go a ' hunting,
> For fear of little men.

Dante Gabriel Rossetti, 'The Maids of Elfen Mere'. *The most famous of Rossetti's illustrations for William Allingham's poems 'The Music Master'. This illustration influenced many other Victorian fairy illustrators, notably Burne-Jones, Frederick Sandys, and Walter Crane. Rossetti's only other fairy illustrations were for his sister's poem, 'Goblin Market' (1862)*

This is one of the most important Victorian fairy poems, and many of Allingham's descriptions of the 'wee folk' correspond exactly to fairies in Victorian paintings and illustrations, particularly the work of Richard Doyle. It was Allingham who provided the text for Doyle's most famous work, 'In Fairy Land' published by Longman's in 1870. Allingham's text is in the form of a play about fairies, including Klingoling, a fairy lutanist, a fairy Princess and her three unwelcome suitors, and sundry fairies including Rosling and Jinkling. In the end the fairy Princess marries a handsome prince, the son and heir of the King of the Blue Mountains.

The 1860s saw the publication of some of the best-known Victorian fairy tales. Christina Rossetti's 'Goblin Market' was published in 1862, a dark and disturbing tale of goblins selling addictive fruit. Her brother Dante Gabriel provided two of its illustrations. In 1863 came Charles Kingsley's 'The Water Babies', telling how Tom, a chimney sweep, escapes and joins the underwater fairies in their marine world. This was a great Victorian favourite, and went through many editions, one

Adelaide Claxton, 'Wonderland'. *Claxton developed a speciality of watercolours showing children in a room with ghostly apparitions hovering around them. By candlelight, this little girl is reading 'Grimm's Fairy Tales', many of which could be scary for children. Ghostly figures hover above, clearly terrifying the cat. Among the other books on the table is 'The Arabian Nights' another Victorian favourite.*

illustrated by Noel Paton, and another by the cartoonist Linley Sambourne. Lewis Carroll's 'Alice's Adventures in Wonderland' was published in 1865. Although it contains no fairies, Carroll had thought of entitling it 'Alice in Elfland', and its characters clearly belong to the fairy world. The same could be said of 'Through the Looking Glass' (1872). Both were illustrated by John Tenniel.

Another popular illustrator of children's books in the mid-Victorian period was Eleanor Vere Boyle, known as EVB. Her illustrations to nursery rhymes were praised by Ruskin and compared to work by Millais and Holman Hunt. She illustrated several books, including 'The Story without an End' (1870), Hans Christian Andersen's 'Fairy Tales' (1873) and 'Beauty and the Beast' (1875). Her illustrations are mostly of children, but fairies do make an appearance in some of the plates, which were printed using the new technique of chromolithography.

Also popular in the late Victorian period were the children's books illustrated by Walter Crane. These were small, eight-page colour books with wood engravings produced for the mass market and sold for sixpence. Some were written as well as illustrated by Crane, such as 'A Song of Sixpence'. Crane's work combines a Pre-Raphaelite effect with an awareness of the Japanese wood-block print with its emphasis on flat areas of colour. Crane illustrated many other books, including Oscar Wilde's 'The Happy Prince' (1888), Spenser's 'Faerie Queene' (1894) and designed fairy costumes and sets for 'The Snowman' by Arthur Sturgess, staged at the Lyceum in 1899.

Crane was the perfect illustrator of the Aesthetic Movement. His work was pretty, charming and decorative, but avoided anything controversial or shocking, or that might be unsuitable for children. He is part of the trend towards prettiness that overtakes later Victorian fairy painting and illustration. The same could be said of Kate Greenaway's work. Her delightful books are mostly about children, but her style influenced many other fairy illustrators, such as Winifred Margaret Tarrant, Cecily Mary Barker and Mabel Lucie Attwell.

Andrew Lang's series of fairy books, beginning with 'The Blue Fairy Book' of 1889, were a tremendous success, and to be found in every Edwardian child's nursery. They ended in 1910 with 'The Lilac Fairy Book'. The illustrations were mostly by Henry Justice Ford; his work influenced the ceramic decorator Daisy Makeig-Jones, and many of Ford's designs are found in her Wedgwood Fairyland Lustre. The Birmingham School also produced many fine illustrators who worked for commercial publishers as well as the many private presses, of which the most influential was William Morris' Kelmscott Press.

Later Victorian authors also wrote about fairies. W.B. Yeats' poem 'The Stolen Child' (1886) is based on the familiar theme of a child abducted by fairies. Yeats also wrote 'Fairy and Folk Tales of Ireland' (1892) in which he enlists the fairies in the cause of Irish nationalism. George MacDonald's Gothic tale 'The Princess and the Goblin' was published in 1872. MacDonald wrote: 'I do not write for

FAIRY LITERATURE

children, but for the child like, whether of five, or fifty, or seventy-five'.

The same could not be said of the Edwardians. By the turn of the century, the emphasis had shifted entirely to the world of children. Fairy painting had by this time died out, and survived only in the world of children's book illustrations. With J.M Barrie's 'Peter Pan', first published as a play in 1904, fairies have very definitely been relegated to the nursery, as has Kenneth Grahame's 'The Wind in the Willows' of 1908. This was the golden age of children's books, and fairies are by this time safely enclosed between book covers and thus rendered harmless. The Edwardian fairy story was a world of whimsy, of entertaining but generally sentimental stories, a world away from the Brothers Grimm and Hans Christian Andersen. The first film version of 'Cinderella' appeared in 1907, and Walt Disney continued the trend towards the prettification and trivialisation of the fairy world, which continues to this day.

The greatest of the Edwardian illustrators was Arthur Rackham (1867–1939), whose work still contains an element of the macabre and the mysterious, unlike most of his contemporaries. In Rackham's illustrations, the fairy world can still be threatening. Rackham developed a highly linear and intricate style, which combines the influence of Cruikshank with that of Dürer and German engravers. He illustrated many of the great children's classics, and it was he who first illustrated Barrie's 'Peter Pan in Kensington Gardens' in 1906. His other great works include 'Rip van Winkle' (1905) and Kipling's 'Puck of Pook's Hill' (1906). There were many other fine Edwardian illustrators of children's books and fairies, such as Edmund Dulac, Jessie M. King, Charles Robinson and William Heath Robinson, but none of them penetrated the fairy world with such a striking mixture of fantasy and reality as Rackham. After the First World War, Rackham found there was less interest in fairy stories, and less demand for his work. He did not go to Hollywood, unlike his fellow illustrator Kay Nielsen who worked on the Mussorgsky sequence in Disney's 'Fantasia', nor was he consulted directly; but Rackham's family remain convinced that he was consulted about Disney's first animated film, 'Snow White'.

One of the offshoots of the Victorian passion for spiritualism was spirit photography, which enjoyed a vogue from the 1870s onwards. This was a photograph in to which an angelic figure or a departed loved one was introduced in the background. In spite of the blatant fraudulence of these photographs, the Victorians were fascinated by them, so great was their desire to get in touch with the spirit world. One photographic firm, Silvestre & Co., advertised among their 'visionary delights – Full luminous female form and dress (with face that convinces) which can be produced in ordinary room or circle, appear gradually, float about room and disappear. Nothing superior'.

Inevitably spirit photography spilled over into the world of fairies. In 1917 the two Cottingley sisters claimed to have seen fairies, producing photographs to

Arthur Rackham, 'The Introduction'. *Rackham was the greatest of the Edwardian illustrators, chosen by J.M. Barrie to illustrate 'Peter Pan in Kensington Gardens'.*

prove it. At this late date, their revelations still caused a sensation, and the controversy surrounding them raged for some years. In 1922, no less a figure than Sir Arthur Conan Doyle, creator of Sherlock Holmes, came to the defence of the girls in his book 'The Coming of the Fairies'. Geoffrey Hodson, a clairvoyant, went with the girls to their 'fairy glen' and claimed that he, too, had seen a group of lovely female fairies dancing, led by a fairy queen 'probably two feet high, surrounded by transparent flowing drapery. There is a star on her forehead, and she has large wings which glisten with pale, delicate shades from pink and lavender…Her hair is golden brown and, unlike that of the lesser fairies, streams behind her and merges with the flowing forces of her aura'. This sounds much the kind of image to be adopted later by Walt Disney and Hollywood. Indeed it still survives today in the world of pantomime. If fairy painting had died out by the 1920s, clearly interest in fairies had not. And judging by the number of books on the subject being produced today, interest in fairies is as great as ever.

CHAPTER THREE

FAIRY THEATRE

Far right: Charles Rolt, 'Prospero relating his history to Miranda'. *Rolt (fl.1845–67) was a painter of mythologies and biblical subjects, and this seems practically his only foray in to fairyland. Predictably he has chosen Shakespeare's 'The Tempest', Act 1. His style owes much to the example of William Etty and W.E. Frost.*

Every time a child says 'I don't believe in fairies' there is a little fairy somewhere that falls down dead

J. M. BARRIE
'PETER PAN', 1904

Fairies in the nineteenth century were inseparable from the theatre. They appeared in plays, ballet, opera and pantomime, and not only provided the fairy painters with inspiration and subject matter, but also shaped the way they depicted fairies. Inevitably, Shakespeare enjoyed a higher status in England than opera or ballet, and it was predictable that his two plays, 'A Midsummer Night's Dream' and 'The Tempest' should inspire so many pictures. Up to about 1860, almost every fairy picture is based on one or other of the plays.

In spite of Hazlitt's warning that 'the boards of a theatre and the regions of fancy are not the same thing', there was no lack of productions of 'The Dream' and 'The Tempest' throughout the whole of the Victorian period. Most combined music, dance, scenic display and spoken drama with the use of technical tricks and special effects. The Victorians also tried as far as possible to return to Shakespeare's original texts. The Victorian approach to both plays was to use scenic effects to the maximum to create an atmosphere of fantasy and magic. This attempt to fuse reality and fantasy is exactly the same as the Victorian painters' desire to depict the fairy world in the greatest possible detail.

The two most famous actor-managers of the early Victorian period were William Charles Macready (1793–1873) and Charles Kean (1811–68), both of

FAIRY THEATRE

FAIRY THEATRE

John Anster Fitzgerald, 'Titania and Bottom, a scene from A Midsummer Night's Dream'. *Fitzgerald usually painted pure fairy subjects, free of any literary association. In depicting the love scene between Titania and Bottom, he has paid homage to the greatest of fairy subjects. In the corners weird figures lurk: to the left an owl confronts goblins; on the right two winged fairies pursue an insect; above, a bat-eared Puck looks on grinning.*

whom made many productions of Shakespeare. Macready staged 'The Tempest' in 1838 using the original text more or less free of earlier alterations and additions. The production was much praised for its exotic effects, evoking the magical atmosphere of Prospero's island. Ariel was generally played by a woman in the nineteenth century, and Macready's Ariel was Priscilla Horton who, as we have seen, created a sensation by flying about the stage on wires and was painted in the role by Daniel Maclise.

Oberon and Puck were also generally played by women, and the popular singer and actress Elizabeth Vestris took the role of Oberon in her production of 'The Dream' in 1840. A critic described her costume:

> She wore a translucent, star-flecked dress of yellow and gold descending only to the knee, tightly belted at the waist, and pinned at the shoulders, exposing arms and neck. Her large eyes were framed by a plumed Grecian helmet with moth-like wings appended, and she carried a gold spear topped with a butterfly.

Madame Vestris was famous for her racy love-life and erotic allure, and never wasted an opportunity to show off her much-admired legs. Prints of her in the role emphasise that for the Victorians fairies were sex symbols. This is the point at which Victorian theatre comes dangerously close to pantomime and burlesque. Victorian fairy painters could be much more explicit, depicting naked fairies and amorous couplings that would have been out of the question on the Victorian stage.

Charles Kean staged lavish productions of 'The Dream' in 1856 and 'The Tempest' in 1857. In 'The Dream' Kean broke with tradition, and cast the eight-year-old Ellen Terry as Puck. From then on it became *de rigueur* to have a young girl in the role. Following Vestris' lead, Kean provided an Athenian classical cityscape for the opening and closing acts. He also went to great lengths to make his costumes, properties and settings historically accurate, just as the Victorian historical painters, such as W.P. Frith or E.M. Ward, would have done. Kean even claimed archaeological sources for the furniture and tools in Quince's workshop 'copies from discoveries at Herculaneum'. The fairies in Kean's production, with their white dresses and wings, looked very much like the peris, sylphs or wilis of romantic ballet. The critics were enthusiastic, and praised the scenery and lavish effects, which were generally thought to heighten the dream-like atmosphere. Several reviewers compared the production to the pictures of Noel Paton and Landseer, an indication of the similarity at the time between fairy painting and fairy theatre.

Kean's production of 'The Tempest' in 1857 was equally sumptuous, with highly exotic scenery and effects, achieved with 'the aid of above one hundred

Daniel Maclise, 'Priscilla Horton as Ariel' (1838–9). William Macready's celebrated production of 'The Tempest' opened at the Theatre Royal, Covent Garden, on 13 October 1838. The magnificence of the staging and the attention to detail were universally acclaimed, but the star of the show was Miss Priscilla Horton, who played Ariel, flying on wires high above the stage. Maclise's picture of her emphasises her shapely figure and statuesque proportions, which seem somewhat unsuitable for the role, but clearly the Victorians liked their Ariels to be substantial.

George Cruikshank, 'Queen Mab'. *An illustration to Mercutio's speech in 'Romeo and Juliet' when he described Queen Mab:*

In shape no bigger than an agate-stone
On the forefinger of an alderman,
Drawn with a team of little atomies
Athwart men's noses as they lie asleep…

and forty operatives nightly', all unseen by the audience. Once again Kean announced that the costumes and the ship were copied from thirteenth century designs and that other mythological details were taken from Greek legends. Kean's Ariel was played by the thirteen-year-old Kate Terry, dressed to appear as like a celestial fairy as possible. Hans Christian Andersen attended the first performance with Dickens, and described Ariel's entrance:

> As Prospero called him forth, a shooting star fell from heaven and touched the turf; it shone in blue and green flame, in which one suddenly saw Ariel's beautiful, angelic form. All in white he stood, with wings from his shoulders to the ground. It was as though, in an instant, he had swung through space on a stellar meteor.

This description seems almost as if Kean had anticipated 'Star Wars' by over a hundred years. Prospero, like a twentieth century spaceship commander, has 'beamed down' Ariel from outer space. These kinds of theatrical effects are certainly to be found in the fairy paintings of Robert Huskisson, Richard Dadd and Noel Paton.

Highly elaborate staging and a lavish degree of visual illusion continued to characterise the Victorian theatre to the end of the century. Herbert Beerbohm Tree's 1904 production of 'The Tempest', for example, continues Kean's use of ornate sets and illusionistic effects, though by this time the critics are beginning to complain that the production was too elaborate and artificial. Clearly taste was at last beginning to change. Harley Granville Barker's 1914 production of 'The Dream' marked a deliberate break from the artificiality and trickery of Victorian theatre towards a new, more realistic and straightforward style.

In the late Victorian period, it became fashionable in aesthetic circles to revive the masque. This was an elaborate court entertainment, made fashionable in the Jacobean age, combining music, dance, and costume. The Art Worker's Guild staged several of these masques, with contributions from many of the leading designers of the day, including Walter Crane, C.R. Ashbee and Henry Wilson. The success of these masques led the aesthetic impresario J. Comyns Carr, who had been one of the founders of the Grosvenor Gallery, to persuade Walter Crane to design the costumes for 'The Snowman', an elaborate Christmas entertainment at the Lyceum. In the final transformation scene, the stage is populated by a new breed of aesthetic fairies: architects and builders, painters, weavers, potters, carpenters and jewellers, all in costumes designed by Crane, each fairy holding a suitable attribute. This was pantomime raised to a new highbrow and aesthetic level.

But fairy theatre was by no means dead, and lived on into the twentieth century. The year 1904 saw the first performance of what is possibly the most

FAIRY THEATRE

FAIRY THEATRE

popular fairy story of all time, J.M Barrie's 'Peter Pan', loved by generations of English children ever since. The full title was 'Peter Pan, or the Boy who wouldn't grow up', thus emphasising that fairies now belonged firmly in the nursery. The plot combined fairyland with crocodiles, piracy, Red Indians and adoption. The exciting new invention of electricity was used to represent the fairy Tinker Bell, a wandering spot of light, accompanied by the sound of bells, 'the fairy language'. It is a simple, but amazingly effective device, which still has audiences spellbound today. 'Peter Pan' also gave us a phrase that has become part of the language: 'Do you believe in fairies?...if you do, clap your hands!' 'Peter Pan' is part of the Edwardian trend towards the increasing prettification and sentimentalisation of the fairy world, a trend to be emphasised further by the early cinema and Walt Disney. Fairies had now become cute and loveable, but harmless, a stereotype that was to persist for the rest of the twentieth century. It could hardly be further from the world of Victorian fairy painting, which was definitely for grown-ups.

Above: Edward Henry Corbould, 'A Fairy Scene, Rothkappchen' (1855). *Corbould (1815–1905) was commissioned by Prince Albert to record a play performed by his children in 1855. The watercolour depicts a tableau at the end of the performance. The Prince of Wales played the Wolf, and Queen Victoria wrote that 'he did his part... particularly well, for it was very difficult'.*

Left: John Anster Fitzgerald 'The Birds' Nest'. *Fairies were always close to the world of animals, especially birds.*

CHAPTER FOUR

FAIRY BALLET

Far right: Edmund Thomas Parris, 'The Visit at Moonlight' (1832). *The connections between romantic ballet and fairy painting are clearly illustrated here. The white, floating figure of a fairy ballerina was transposed to many a Victorian fairy painting, becoming a potent and much-repeated image.*

The Victorian period was to see many productions of Shakespeare's 'A Midsummer Night's Dream' and 'The Tempest', all of which undoubtedly inspired the fairy painters. But the emergence of the romantic ballet was to have an equally important effect. Fairies have always been associated with music and dancing, but it was from the ballet that the Victorian painters of fairies took their imagery.

The greatest ballerina of the early Victorian period was Madame Marie Taglioni, who is generally credited with first dancing on points. Her ability to waft effortlessly across the stage in an ethereal, fairy-like way caused a sensation, and it was she who made famous most of the romantic ballets of the period. Her first appearance in London was in 1830, in Charles Didelot's ballet 'Flore et Zéphyr'. This was followed two years later by 'La Sylphide', which was to be her greatest success. Set in Scotland, it tells a Walter Scott-like romantic story of a mortal man torn between his love for his betrothed, Effie, and a fairy. The critics were ecstatic, and Madame Taglioni took London by storm. The French critic Théophile Gautier had already written how she:

> Flies like a spirit in the midst of the transparent clouds of muslin with which she loves to surround herself…

The portrait painter Alfred Edward Chalon (1780–1860) made a set of six charming watercolours of Taglioni, which were then published as lithographs

(overleaf). Through these prints, and her performances in other roles, Taglioni was to be the prototype of many a fairy queen or nymph in Victorian painting.

It was Gautier who devised the plot of 'Giselle', the most famous of romantic ballets, which was first performed in 1841. Based on a poem by Heine, and featuring the wilis, the ghosts of girls who have died before their wedding days, it has remained in the repertoire ever since. Other romantic ballets with fairy themes include 'Ondine', danced by Fanny Cerrito in 1843 and composed and

FAIRY BALLET

Circle of Richard Doyle, 'The Dance of the Pixies'. *Almost all folklore contains descriptions of fairies dancing; it seems to have been a favourite pastime, and humans who witnessed it would often be drawn in to the dance, as by a spell. Many fairy pictures show fairies dancing; inevitably their poses and movements echo those of the ballet.*

Right: Alfred Edward Chalon, 'Marie Taglioni in La Sylphide' (1845). *'La Sylphide' was first performed in London on 26 July 1832 to enormous acclaim, and it set the seal on the new vogue for romantic ballet. Its star, Marie Taglioni, played a fairy, with whom the hero, James, falls in love and deserts his fiancée. He presents La Sylphide with a birds' nest; alarmed, she flies to the tree tops to replace it. This is one of six watercolours by Chalon of Taglioni in the role; all six were later published as lithographs in 1845, to mark Taglioni's retirement.*

choreographed by Jules Perrot, whose next ballet, entitled 'Eoline, ou la Dryade' (1845), was a tragic tale in which Eoline, half-human and half-dryad, dies on her wedding day at the hand of the jealous Rubezahl, the prince of the gnomes.

In general, major composers did not write for the ballet in the nineteenth century. However, Tchaikovsky composed the music for 'Sleeping Beauty' (1890) and 'The Nutcracker Suite' (1892), both of which featured many types of fairies. Most famous of the roles was that of the Sugar Plum Fairy in 'The Nutcracker Suite', whose music was specially composed on a new instrument, the celesta. But Victorian audiences would not have known these ballets, which were only brought to England by Diaghilev in the 1920s.

Fairies were also an integral feature of that most English of entertainment, the pantomime. During the Victorian period, the pantomime was at the height of its popularity, and many artists, designers and writers worked for it. The stage settings and special effects rivalled those of the theatre and ballet, and fairies both flew through the air on wires and appeared from trap doors in the stage. Fairies also traditionally appeared in 'transformation' scenes, in which gauze screens were lifted one by one to reveal an imaginary world beyond, and scenes with these effects were frequently used as finales. All of these pantomime illusions provided the fairy painter with further sources of inspiration over and above those offered by the theatre and ballet.

In the Victorian period, the fairy world was inseparable from the stage, and when painters came to depict fairy subjects, it was images from theatre and ballet which provided the inspiration for their pictures.

FAIRY BALLET

Richard Doyle, 'The Attar Cup in Aagerup – the Moment of Departure'. *The subject is from Danish mythology, and was taken by Doyle from Thomas Keightley's 'The Fairy Mythology' of 1828. The story tells of a farmer's servant in the village of Aagerup who spends a night with the trolls. As day breaks, he mounts his horse and is invited to drink a stirrup cup, or attar cup, before he departs. To the right, the trolls dance in a ring; in their white dresses they look as if they might have come straight out of a romantic ballet.*

Robert Alexander Hillingford, 'The Fairy Dance'. *Hillingford (1825–1904) was best-known as a military and historical painter, especially of Napoleonic battles. This rare departure for him is an indication of the popularity of fairy subjects in the mid-Victorian period. The subject is a fairy dance, or fairy ring, set in a wood, with various insects hovering around.*

FAIRY BALLET

CHAPTER FIVE

Fairy Music

Far right: Follower of Sir Joseph Noel Paton, 'Fairy Music'. *Many sightings of fairies in folklore involved not only fairy dancing, but also fairy music. Clearly this young girl is listening to fairies playing the harp, bells and other instruments as they flit about the sky above her.*

Fairies inspired many nineteenth century composers, from Weber to Gilbert and Sullivan, and were featured in opera as well as ballet. Weber was the first to turn 'A Midsummer Night's Dream' into an opera, which he entitled 'Oberon, or the Elf-King's Oath' (1826). His score was greatly admired by the boy genius, Felix Mendelssohn. 'A Midsummer Night's Dream' was the Mendelssohn family's favourite play, often read and performed by them at home. Inspired both by the play and by Weber's 'Oberon', Mendelssohn composed his 'A Midsummer Night's Dream Overture,' a dazzling *tour de force*, which remains the finest piece of fairy music ever written.

Berlioz, both a friend and admirer of Mendelssohn, was inspired by 'A Midsummer Night's Dream Overture' to write a scherzo on the theme of Shakespeare's Queen Mab speech in 'Romeo and Juliet'. This he included in his choral symphony 'Romeo and Juliet' (1839). Berlioz also wrote an overture to 'The Tempest' in 1830. This he later incorporated in the 'Symphonie Fantastique', and then rewrote for 'The Damnation of Faust' of 1846. Various other composers made sorties into the fairy world, including Wagner, whose first opera, 'Die Feen', was written in 1834 but never produced in his lifetime. Much more successful was Verdi's last opera 'Falstaff'. In the final scene Falstaff is lured in to Windsor Forest, where he is surrounded by apparitions, pinched and tormented by elves, imps and fairies, who are in fact the Merry Wives and their families in disguise.

FAIRY MUSIC

FAIRY MUSIC

Above: John Anster Fitzgerald, 'Fairy Musicians'. *Fairies traditionally made music and taught birds to sing. Here fairies and birds sing to the accompaniment of a snowdrop lute.*

Right: Arthur Rackham, 'A Fairy Song' *A drawing for his 1930 edition of 'A Midsummer Night's Dream', but not used. Titania sleeps while her attendants gather in a tree:*

Sing me now asleep;
Then to your offices, and let me rest.

Inevitably, the great English duo, Gilbert and Sullivan, decided to turn their attention to the world of fairies. Following their success with 'Patience' in 1880, a satire on the critics of the high Victorian aesthetes, and the world of the 'greenery-yallery Grosvenor Gallery', in 1882 they produced a new operetta, 'Iolanthe, or the Peer and the Peri'. Described as 'An entirely new and original Fairy Opera', Gilbert contrived to link fairies with the emerging suffragette movement, threatening the House of Lords:

> We are dainty little fairies,
> Ever singing, ever dancing;
> We indulge in our vagaries
> In a fashion most entrancing.
> If you ask the special function
> Of our never-ceasing motion,
> We reply, without compunction,
> That we haven't any notion.

Contemporaries thought that Iolanthe, the Fairy Queen, whose costume strongly resembled that of Wagner's Brünnhilde, represented Queen Victoria, the Lord Chancellor was Gladstone, and Private Willis, a guardsman who attracts Iolanthe's attention, was John Brown, the queen's faithful Highland servant. All this is not as fanciful as it may sound; Disraeli, Queen Victoria's favourite prime minister, always referred to her as 'the Faerie', in a mocking allusion to Spenser's 'Faerie Queene'.

Gilbert's last operatic venture, in 1909, was another operetta entitled 'Fallen Fairies, or The Wicked World'. In spite of the great success of 'Peter Pan' a few years before, 'Fallen Fairies' was a failure. Taste in both fairies, and fairy music had moved on. Even so, Dvorak's 'Rusalka' of 1901, which tells the story of a handsome prince who falls in love with a wood nymph, was a success, and has remained a popular opera ever since.

It seems that fairies are one of those recurring themes that every age has to reinterpret for itself.

CHAPTER SIX

THE
EARLY VICTORIANS

*Fairy Roses, fairy rings,
Turn out sometimes troublesome things.*

W.M. THACKERAY
'THE ROSE AND THE RING', 1855

Theodore von Holst.
'Fairy Lovers' (circa 1840).
The picture illustrates an episode from Goethe's 'Faust'; the lines are from 'A Walpurgis Night's Dream':

*We walk short-stepped but
high of heart,
Through honey-dew and
flowers.
Yes, you can trot with agile art,
But flight is not yet ours.*

After Blake and Fuseli's work of the late eighteenth century there was a pause, and it was not until the 1830s that interest in fairy paintings began to revive, in the work of Edmund Thomas Parris, and the two Irish artists, Francis Danby and Daniel Maclise. Parris (1793–1873), a now forgotten artist, was well-known in his day as a portrait painter, and painted one of the first portraits of Queen Victoria after her coronation. He also painted historical subjects, and the occasional fairy picture, in which the floating white females are strongly reminiscent of the romantic ballet.

Francis Danby (1793-1861) was born in Ireland, but at first settled in Bristol, before eloping to the Continent in 1829, following a matrimonial scandal. During the 1830s, he painted one or two fairy watercolours, on the theme of Oberon and Titania (page 21). Thereafter he only painted one other scene, from 'The Tempest', in 1846. His *forte* was poetic landscape, as demonstrated by *An Enchanted Isle* of 1824, or better known, *The Wood Nymph's Hymn to the Rising Sun* (1845). Another artist of the 1830s to paint 'A Midsummer Night's Dream' was the little-known John Lamb (1798–1873) known as 'Primus', or Lamb the elder.

The contribution of Daniel Maclise (1806–70) to fairy painting was to be far greater than that of Parris or Danby. Maclise first set up a portrait studio in Cork. One of his patrons, Mr. Sainthill, was a local antiquary who allowed him access to

THE EARLY VICTORIANS

Above: Daniel Maclise, 'Undine' (1844). The young knight Huldrand escorts his bride Undine through the forest, followed by a monk; he draws his sword to confront Kühleborn, the spirit of the water, and uncle of Undine, who bars their way. The picture was bought by Queen Victoria at the Royal Academy in 1844, and given to Prince Albert as a birthday present.

Right: James Elliot, 'Fairies playing in a Birds' Nest'. Elliott was unknown as a fairy painter until recently. Obviously familiar with the detailed still lifes of birds' nests by William Henry 'Birds' Nest' Hunt, Elliott seems to have been the first to combine this genre with fairies.

THE EARLY VICTORIANS

his library of books about legends and folklore. He also introduced Maclise to Crofton Croker, the author of 'Fairy Legends and Traditions of the South of Ireland' (1826). Thus by the time he came to London in 1827, Maclise had already acquired some knowledge of fairy folklore. Although he was to become better known as a historical painter, Maclise included several fairy pictures in his repertoire, such as *The Disenchantment of Bottom* of 1832, and *The Faun and the Fairies* of about 1834. The grotesque elements in *Bottom* hark back to Fuseli, whose work Maclise admired. *The Faun* shows Maclise's own remarkable talent emerging, particularly his masterly handling of the circle of flying nude figures

THE EARLY VICTORIANS

Edwin Landseer, 'Scene from A Midsummer Night's Dream, Titania and Bottom' (1848–51). *Landseer's only venture in to fairyland, the painting was commissioned by the great engineer Brunel for a Shakespearean dining-room. Landseer has chosen the moment that offered the greatest opportunity to paint animals, when Titania awakes and falls in love with Bottom transformed into an ass. Queen Victoria thought Landseer's fairy picture a success – 'a gem, beautifully fairy-like and forceful'.*

surrounding the malevolent figure of the faun. Maclise befriended both Dickens and Bulwer Lytton, and illustrated the latter's 'Pilgrims of the Rhine' in 1834 with an engraving of *The Faun and the Fairies*. He also illustrated Thomas Moore's 'Irish Melodies' of 1846 with numerous fairy subjects.

In 1844 Maclise received royal approval for the finest of his fairy pictures, *Undine*, which was purchased at the Royal Academy by Queen Victoria, and given to Prince Albert for his birthday (page 64). The picture is an astonishing *tour de force*, and Albert would certainly have appreciated its strongly Germanic style and colouring, reflecting Maclise's admiration for the German Nazarene painters Schnorr von Carolsfeld and Moritz von Schwind. The immediate inspiration for Maclise's *Undine* was probably the ballet 'Ondine' by Jules Perrot, which was first performed in London the year before in 1843. Both picture and ballet were based on a story by the German writer De La Motte Fouqué. As we have seen, Maclise had painted the actress Priscilla Horton as Ariel, in William Macready's production of 'The Tempest' in 1838 (page 46). This had been a great success, mainly because of the elaborate staging and special effects one of which had Horton flying across the stage on wires while singing 'Merrily, Merrily' suspended in the air.

After *Undine*, Maclise was too occupied with his work on large historical murals in the Houses of Parliament to paint any more fairy pictures. But a number of other artists turned to fairy subjects in the 1840s, notably Turner and Landseer. In 1846 the great Turner exhibited a picture of *Queen Mab's Cave* at the British Institution, but it was not one of his best efforts, and even his admirer Ruskin declared it a failure. Mab was the fairies' midwife, and was described by Shakespeare in Mercutio's speech in 'Romeo and Juliet':

> In shape no bigger than an agate stone
> On the fore-finger of an alderman,
> Drawn with a team of little atomies
> Athwart mens' noses as they lie asleep.
> Her waggon-spokes made of long spinners' legs;
> The cover of the wings of grasshoppers…
> Her waggoner, a small grey-coated gnat…
> Her chariot is an empty hazel-nut
> Made by the joiner squirrel or old grub.

These are the kind of images a fairy painter might have had in mind when he turned to painting the 'little people'.

THE EARLY VICTORIANS

The one and only foray into fairyland made by Sir Edwin Landseer (1802–73) was his *Scene from A Midsummer Night's Dream, Titania and Bottom.* It was commissioned by Isambard Kingdom Brunel for a Shakespearean dining-room in his London house. Typically, Landseer has chosen the scene with Bottom, turned into an ass, being wooed by the enslaved Titania. On the right, two of the numerous fairies are riding on white rabbits. The picture is highly finished, completely realistic, and painted in minute detail. Only a Victorian painter would try and depict the fairy world like this, yet it works because the figures loom out of a dark and mysterious background.

Two other artists also painted fairies in the 1830s, David Scott and Theodore von Holst. Scott (1806–49), the elder brother of the Pre-Raphaelite William Bell

James Elliot, 'Fairies and Fruit'. *Elliott has here combined the William Henry Hunt type of still life of fruit with fairies and cherubs. He appears to be the only still life artist to have done this, and his work represents a unique development in fairy painting.*

Scott, was a painter of grandiose historical scenes, but his work met with little success, and he died a disappointed man aged only forty-three. In 1837 he painted two Shakespearean scenes, *Ariel and Caliban* and *Puck fleeing before the Dawn*. The critics were completely baffled by the visionary intensity, awkward figures and gloomy colouring of both pictures. In style they seem to hark back to Blake and Fuseli, rather than belonging to Victorian art. Difficult though Scott's work is, it is completely original.

Theodore von Holst (1810–44) was a pupil and follower of Fuseli, but like Scott he never enjoyed proper recognition of his considerable talents. One of the few artists to admire him was the young Rossetti. Holst painted scenes from Dante, Scott, Byron, Shakespeare and Goethe, including a number of fairy subjects, such as *Fairy Lovers* (page 62).

Little is known of James Elliot who exhibited landscapes and still lifes at the Royal Academy and the Royal Society of British Artists (1848–73). Indeed, he was unknown as a fairy painter until recently. He was obviously familiar with the detailed still lifes of 'Birds' Nest Hunt', and seems to have been the first to combine this genre with fairies.

THE EARLY VICTORIANS

David Scott, 'Puck fleeing before the Dawn' (1837). *One of the most extraordinary depictions of Puck, curled up in a ball, hurtling through the night sky like a shot from a cannon. In the same year, Scott painted 'Ariel and Caliban', an equally eccentric picture. Clearly 'The Tempest' struck a chord in his imagination.*

CHAPTER SEVEN

ROBERT HUSKISSON
1819–1861

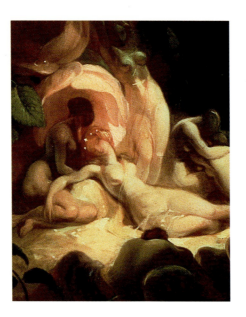

Robert Huskisson, 'The Midsummer Night's Fairies – There sleeps Titania' (1847). *Huskisson was clearly influenced by Dadd's version of the same subject (pages 78 and 79) exhibited in 1841. But Huskisson has introduced elements of his own – the figure of Titania is taken from a Sleeping Psyche by Giulio Romano, in the Sala di Psiche in the Palazzo del Te, Mantua. Huskisson has also used the device of setting the scene in a decorated proscenium arch. Another version of this picture is in the Tate Gallery.*

Huskisson was one of the first Victorian artists to make a speciality of fairy subjects, although few of these survive. Born near Nottingham, Huskisson painted portraits, figurative and historical subjects, and came to London in 1839. During the 1840s he began to exhibit fairy subjects, based on 'A Midsummer Night's Dream' and 'The Tempest'. The finest of these to survive both date from 1847, *The Midsummer Night's Fairies* and *'Come unto these yellow Sands'*. These show Huskisson to be an artist of great lyrical and technical ability, and one of the best Victorian fairy painters.

Both the paintings are highly theatrical, and are set with a painted proscenium arch, as if we are looking at a stage. Both arches are painted and decorated with allegorical figures. The proscenium arch was a standard feature of the Victorian theatre, although Benjamin Wyatt, who designed the Drury Lane theatre of 1811, was insistent that the arch should not distract attention from the stage, any more than a picture should be 'diverted…from the richness of the Picture-frame'. The theatrical settings of Huskisson's pictures emphasise the close connections between fairy painting and the theatre, and one wonders if he had seen any of Macready's productions of Shakespeare. The genre and historical painter W.P. Frith was a keen theatregoer, as were many artists in the early Victorian period. Frith was a friend and admirer of Macready and also knew Huskisson, so may have been a link between the two men.

Stylistically, Huskisson's pictures owe much to the example of William Etty and William Edward Frost, both of whom were influential in the 1840s. Etty was

ROBERT HUSKISSON

71

a painter of classical subjects rather than fairies, but Frost's pictures of nereids and wood nymphs undoubtedly had an influence on fairy painting, especially in the painting of female nudes.

Huskisson must also have seen Richard Dadd's version illustrating the song from 'The Tempest' sung by Ariel, *'Come unto these yellow Sands'*, exhibited at the Royal Academy in 1842. But Huskisson absorbed these influences, and developed a minutely-detailed and highly polished style all his own. His colours are also highly distinctive, with the pearly flesh tones of the figures set against deep blue backgrounds. His lighting is also highly theatrical, seeming to spotlight the main figures in the composition, a feature which must reflect the influence of new developments in the theatre with the introduction of gas lamps and limelight.

Both Huskisson's fairy pictures of 1847 were bought by Samuel Carter Hall, proprietor and editor of the 'Art Union', later the 'Art Journal', and both were engraved in it. Another picture entitled *The Mother's Blessing* was engraved as the frontispiece to 'Midsummer Eve: A Fairy Tale of Love', written by Hall's wife. After Huskisson's early death in 1861, the Halls sent both his pictures to auction, and Hall remarked in his lengthy autobiography that Huskisson had 'slipped out of the world, no-one knew when or how'.

A reference to Huskisson appears in an account in the 'Autobiography' of Frith, in which he describes meeting Huskisson at a dinner given by Lord Northwick, a prominent early Victorian patron, at Thirlestane Manor, Cheltenham. Huskisson had painted a copy of Etty's *Rape of Proserpine* for Northwick. Frith wrote rather waspishly that Huskisson was 'a very common man, entirely uneducated. The very tone of his voice was dreadful', although Frith concedes Huskisson 'had painted some original pictures of considerable merit'. He recalled that Lord Northwick asked: "Mr Huskisson, was it not a picture dealer who bought your last 'Fairy' picture?" "No, my Lord!", replied Huskisson, "It were a gent."

Undoubtedly Huskisson was of humble origin, and spoke with an accent, but two letters written by him survive in the Getty Museum in Los Angeles. They are written in an elegant hand, and contradict Frith's assertion that he was 'entirely uneducated'. A great future was predicted for Huskisson; a critic of the 'Art Union' claimed that he was 'destined to play a premier role in British art'. Sadly, his illness and early death brought these lofty predictions to nought. It was a sad end for the most promising of the fairy painters. One can only hope that more of Huskisson's work will in time come to light.

Robert Huskisson, 'Come unto these yellow Sands' (1847). *Huskisson's pictures clearly underline the connections between fairy painting and the theatre. His use of dramatic lighting is highly theatrical, as is the painted proscenium arch, which gives the viewer the impression of looking at a stage. The composition owes much to Richard Dadd's 1842 version of the same subject (page 77).*

CHAPTER EIGHT

RICHARD DADD
1819–1866

Richard Dadd, 'The Fairy Feller's Master Stroke' (1855–64). Dadd's last great fairy masterpiece, painted between 1855 and 1864. Dadd intended the subject to come purely from the imagination, and wrote a long verse account of how he painted it. Few pictures in art history can have been painted under such extraordinary circumstances. A contemporary described Dadd working at Bethlem Royal Hospital 'amidst the most revolting conversation and the most brutal behaviour'.

Because he went mad, Richard Dadd is the one fairy painter everyone has heard of. He was mad Dadd. He only painted about ten fairy pictures, but two of them, painted after he went mad, are the undoubted masterpieces of the genre. His story is one of the strangest, and most tragic chapters in the history of Victorian art.

Everything about Dadd's early career was perfectly normal, even predictable. He entered the Royal Academy Schools in 1837, and joined a mildly rebellious group of fellow-students, known as 'The Clique'. Its fellow members included Frith and H.N. O'Neil. Dadd's early works were mostly landscapes, animals and still life, of an utterly conventional kind, showing little or no sign of his future promise. It was not until the early 1840s, perhaps under the influence of Maclise, that he began to paint fairy pictures.

Something about the fairy world seems to have struck a chord with Dadd, because his talent immediately began to blossom. In 1841 he painted at least three notable fairy pictures, *Puck*, *The Haunt of the Fairies* (page 80), and *Titania Sleeping*. *Puck* is a circular picture, showing a naked, and rather mischievous figure seated on a toadstool, surrounded by a ring of fairy dancers. The figure of Puck is slightly reminiscent of Reynolds' *Puck* of nearly fifty years earlier, but Dadd has created an altogether different atmosphere, much more mysterious and fantastical.

Puck was shown at the Society of British Artists in 1841, and the 'Art Union' reviewer declared that 'Mr. Dadd is on the right road to fame'. *The Haunt of the*

RICHARD DADD

Richard Dadd, 'Come unto these yellow Sands' (1842). *The last picture exhibited by Dadd before madness changed his life and his career. It was shown at the Royal Academy in 1842, just before his departure to the Middle East. The scene is from 'The Tempest', depicting Ariel's song in Act 1, Scene ii. The daring composition, and troupe of dancing figures, very like ballerinas, were to be much imitated by other fairy painters, notably Maclise and Huskisson.*

Fairies was a less dramatic picture, showing a single kneeling figure of a naked fairy, but it is set against a particularly dramatic sky, with a lurid sunset and a lone star in the twilight.

The third picture, *Titania Sleeping* (overleaf), was the most remarkable of the three, and was shown at the Royal Academy in that same year, 1841. It shows Titania with three attendants being lulled to sleep in her bower of wild thyme, oxlips, violets and woodbine. The flowers encircle her like an arch, and among the flowers is a ring of fairies, gnomes and elves. To the left, larger figures of fairies dance away into the night, and above, a network of interlocking bats' wings forms a kind of proscenium arch. The device of the fairy circle with flowers may well have been borrowed from Maclise's *Undine* or *The Faun and the Fairies*, but Dadd has invested the scene with a dark and mysterious atmosphere all his own. The reviewer of the 'Literary Gazette' thought the picture promised, 'greater efforts to the clever young artist. The conception of the fairy circle boasts of originality, even after the hundreds of times it has been painted...'. Dadd's picture now hangs in the Louvre in Paris, where it is a lone representative of Victorian fairy painting.

These fairy pictures had turned Dadd into a rising star. The proprietor of the 'Art Union', Samuel Carter Hall, commissioned him to illustrate his 'Book of British Ballads', published in two volumes in 1842 and 1844. Dadd only completed four illustrations for the book, all scenes for 'Robin Goodfellow'. The other illustrators included John Tenniel, John Gilbert, Noel Paton, E.H. Corbould and Alfred Crowquill.

In 1842 Dadd exhibited the finest, and what was to be the last, of his early fairy pictures, *'Come unto these yellow Sands'*, a brilliant evocation of Ariel's song in 'The Tempest', with which he lures Ferdinand to his meeting with Miranda:

> Come unto these yellow sands,
> And then take hands.
> Curtsied when you have and kissed
> The wild waves whist,
> Foot it featly here and there;
> And, sweet sprites, the burden bear.

This was the scene to be depicted, very differently, by Millais in 1849, with his *Ferdinand Lured by Ariel* (page 143). Dadd has chosen to paint neither Ferdinand nor Ariel, but a ring of dancing sprites coming down from the sky, footing it featly through a rocky arch on a deserted coast. This time Dadd has created something altogether more original and fantastical, and the critics were unanimously enthusiastic. The 'Art Union' thought it captured 'more nearly the essence of the poet than any other illustration we have seen'. The spiralling group

of cherubs and nymphs coming out of a dark, twilit sky was a brilliant touch, to be imitated later in the 1840s by Robert Huskisson (page 72). The dramatic lighting of the dancing figures is highly theatrical, and the sprites trip like ballerinas on their points. All this suggests that the ballet may have been Dadd's inspiration, although we do not know if he ever saw Taglioni in 'La Sylphide'.

It was later in the same year, 1842, that Richard Dadd embarked on what is now seen as his fateful trip to the Middle East. Encouraged by his friend, the

RICHARD DADD

Richard Dadd, 'Titania Sleeping' (circa 1841). Exhibited at the Royal Academy in 1841 with a quotation from Oberon's speech Act II, Scene ii:

There sleeps Titania sometime of the night
Lull'd in the flowers with dances and delight.

This was the finest of Dadd's fairy pictures painted before his madness. The composition echoes both Giorgione's 'Adoration of the Shepherds' and Poussin's 'Bacchanals', showing that even Victorian fairy painting is part of the European tradition.

RICHARD DADD

Scottish painter, David Roberts, Dadd joined the retinue of Sir Thomas Phillips, who he later painted in Arab dress smoking a hookah. Together they travelled to Venice, Corfu, Greece, the Levant, and up the Nile to Thebes. The many watercolours Dadd executed on his travels have a manic intensity that presaged what was to come. In a letter to his friend Frith, Dadd wrote prophetically: 'At times the excitement of these scenes has been enough to turn the brains of an ordinary weak-minded person like myself, and often I have lain down at night with my imagination so full of wild vagaries that I have really and truly doubted my own sanity'. Dadd's travelling companion noticed that he was beginning to have delusions, and sent him home ahead.

On his return to London in 1843, all at first seemed well. Dadd entered the Westminster competitions to decorate Barry and Pugin's new Houses of Parliament but his picture of St. George was rejected because the dragon's tail was too long. Shortly after this, his father took him to the country on the advice of a doctor. While staying overnight at Cobham, Dadd inexplicably stabbed and killed his father and then fled to France. His intention was to murder the Emperor of Austria, but he succeeded only in stabbing a fellow passenger on the diligence at Fontainbleau, before he was arrested and brought back to England. Dadd confessed that he believed his father was the devil and that his mission as an envoy of the God Osiris was to 'exterminate the men most possessed with the demon'.

Dadd spent the rest of his life in mental institutions, first the Bethlem Royal Hospital, then Broadmoor. The 'Art Union' wrote of him in 1843: 'The late Richard Dadd. Alas! We must so preface the name of a youth of genius that promised to do honour to the world; for, although the grave has not actually closed over him, he must be classed among the dead'. At Bethlem, Dadd was fortunate in having a humane and tolerant governor, Dr. William Charles Hood, who supplied him with painting and drawing materials and encouraged him to continue painting. So Dadd may have been dead to the world, but his career was not yet over. His output at Bethlem was not large. Eleven drawings, dating from 1854, survive in the Bethlem Royal Hospital, of varying quality, but all characterised by a degree of obsessiveness. He did however complete two major pictures, which are among the finest of Victorian fairy pictures – *Contradiction: Oberon and Titania* (1854–8) and *The Fairy Feller's Master Stroke* (1855–64). Both are completely different in style and colouring from Dadd's fairy subjects of the 1840s. These are fairy paintings of a madman, yet by all accounts Dadd was a gentle and harmless character, as revealed in a photograph of him at work.

Contradiction: Oberon and Titania (overleaf) is an oval shape, unusual for a fairy painting, and unusual for Dadd. In conception it is an extraordinary mixture of the real and the fantastical, and is characterised by a relentless accumulation of detail over the whole of the picture's surface. The main figures are depicted as if life size, in contrast to the tiny fairies and other weird creatures around them. In

Richard Dadd, 'The Haunt of the Fairies' (circa 1841). *One of the small group of fairy pictures painted by Dadd in the early 1840s, before he went mad in 1843. These works show Dadd to have been a talented, if conventional, fairy painter; his madness was to transform him into the most remarkable of fairy painters.*

the centre stand Oberon and Titania, dressed in vaguely classical robes, as if they were representing Theseus and Hippolyta. Oberon with his dark beard and curious helmet, looks like the Syrian sheikh that Dadd recalled meeting on his Middle Eastern travels. Beside him stands a malevolent-looking Puck, with a fantastical jester's head-dress and wings. Behind Oberon is a train of exotically dressed followers, with further back a group of bacchanalian revellers and a satyr depicted in the style of a Roman procession. Behind Titania, who wears an amazingly spiky and theatrical crown, cowers the changeling Indian boy, the source of the quarrel. He wears a Russian-looking conical hat that looks as if it came out of a pantomime. To the right stand one of the pairs of lovers in the play, Demetrius and Helena, who have entered somewhat ahead of their cue. They too are in classical robes, though Helena wears a large yellow hat. Their faces are fixed and expressionless, as are those of Oberon and Titania, and they stand as if frozen motionless in a tableau, static and immobile. There is no sense of movement or interplay between the figures, only fixed stares, as if glaring at each other. The atmosphere is arid and airless, emphasised by the mainly grey and brown colours, and adds to the prevailing feeling of tension and unease.

Around the central figures is a tapestry of dun-coloured leaves, flowers and foliage. On a leaf in the foreground is a jewelled blue butterfly; in the background is a large green egg, delicately balanced on an elegant metal stand; nearby are other similar stands, and a terrestrial globe. The drooping convolvulus in the centre suggests that the action is meant to take place at night, yet the picture is bathed in an artificially even light, as if the scene was taking place on stage. Among the leaves and grasses are numerous fairies, one intervening to prevent an arrow being fired at Titania, and other goblins and beasts, some half-human, half-animal. Dewdrops are scattered at random over the surface. The picture is an extraordinary *tour de force*, by any standards, and not surprisingly it took at least four years to paint. As a result, it inevitably looks laboured and static, but it is one of the greatest of fairy pictures, as well as one of the curiosities of English nineteenth century art.

Much the same could be said of Dadd's other Bethlem masterpiece, *The Fairy Feller's Master Stroke* (page 75). This took nine years to paint, and is in many ways a more remarkable picture. This time, the subject is not literary, but pure fantasy. In Dadd's own account, he tried to eliminate his imagination and so

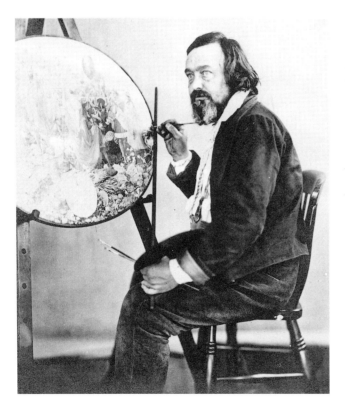

Fairy painter and madman. Photograph of Richard Dadd painting 'Contradiction' in Bethlem Royal Hospital (circa 1856). It was while he was confined to mental institutions that Dadd painted his two fairy masterpieces, 'Contradiction', and 'The Fairy Feller's Master Stroke'.

Richard Dadd, 'Contradiction: Oberon and Titania' (1854–8). *Dadd's masterpiece, and one of the greatest of fairy pictures. Dadd did not begin the picture until he had been in Bethlem Royal Hospital for ten years; he then worked on it for four years and dedicated it to the governor of the hospital, Dr. William Charles Hood, who encouraged Dadd to continue painting. The picture was never shown in Dadd's lifetime, and not exhibited in public until 1930.*

The figures of Demetrius and Helena, above, and, right, a jewel-like blue butterfly, details from Dadd's painting 'Contradiction: Oberon and Titania'.

gazed at the canvas and thought of nothing, 'until pure fancy began to give form to the cloudy paint he had already smeared over it'. This time the colour scheme is much darker, with dark green, grey and brown predominating. The foreground is a web of grasses, through which the spectator has to look, as if peering into a fairy world. Once again, the figures vary considerably in size, and are scattered all over the picture, set against a flat, tapestry-like field of leaves, grasses and white daisies. Even more than *Contradiction*, *The Fairy Feller* has the trance-like, hallucinatory quality of a dream-world, this time even more weird, obsessive and menacing.

Dadd dedicated the picture to G.H. Haydon, who was Dr. Hood's assistant at Bethlem, and also wrote a long verse account of how he painted the picture, entitled 'Elimination of a Picture and its Subject'. In this he explains all the characters in the picture, most of whom seem to be waiting expectantly for the fairy feller in the foreground to swing his axe and split the hazel nut in front of him. Other hazel nuts are scattered on the ground behind him. In the very centre of the picture is a white-bearded old man, a patriarchal figure with a papal triple crown. He is the magician controlling events, and his right hand is raised to command the fairy feller: 'Except I tell you when, strike if you dare'. In his left hand he holds a club for hitting small fairies over the head. As a figure, he is highly reminiscent of the bearded god-like figures of William Blake. The other characters in the picture are a curious mixture, and although they purport to come purely from Dadd's imagination, they are curiously reminiscent of the grotesque caricatures to be found in the work of illustrators such as George Cruikshank and Richard Doyle. As a cast of characters, they seem to have stepped out of a slightly grotesque version of 'Punch', or the novels of Dickens. They come deliberately from all walks of life: on the right are two elegant men-about-town in vaguely seventeenth century costume and plumed hats;

in the centre a dandy is flirting with a winged nymph; beside them crouches an anxious-looking pedagogue. To the left are two strangely dressed maids, one holding a mirror, the other a broom. The one on the left has enormously bulbous calves and a bodice accentuating her pointy breasts. Further back, in the centre, are Oberon and Titania wearing crowns, with a tiny witch in a Welsh hat beside them. Below, a tiny procession passes with Queen Mab in her coach drawn by female centaurs, with a gnat as coachman perched on the brim of the patriarch's hat. At the top of the picture is another curious array of figures. To the left is a dragonfly playing a trumpet, and another figure blowing an elaborate horn. Dadd describes him as 'a tatterdemalion and a junketer, Holiday folk'. To their right are figures from nursery rhyme: soldier, sailor, tinker, tailor, ploughboy, apothecary, thief. The tinker stands by a bizarre wheelbarrow-like contraption; the apothecary looks very like Dadd's father; the soldier is a Napoleonic dwarf. Below the trumpet-playing dragonfly an elf wearing a red conical hat peeps through the grass. Dadd explains that he is 'of the Chinese Small Foot Societee, He's a small member'. All the figures are of varying sizes, which adds to the illusion that we are looking in to a strange fairy world, distorted by dreams. Scale and perspective shift as our eye moves over the picture in which every inch of surface is covered and carefully worked out, like a tapestry or embroidery.

Detail of the fairy feller in Dadd's strange fairy world.

Like *Contradiction, The Fairy Feller* is one of the great oddities of Victorian painting. It is more often compared to the Flemish artist Hieronymus Bosch than to Dadd's own contemporaries. Yet the figures are a motley, Dickensian throng, and unmistakably Victorian. Although Dadd claimed the picture was 'pure fancy', the figures all have an artistic or literary pedigree of some kind. It is the fairy equivalent of Ford Madox Brown's *Work*, painted by a madman.

Dadd died in Broadmoor in 1886, aged sixty-six. Although some of his earlier pictures were exhibited during his lifetime, neither *Contradiction* nor *The Fairy Feller* were seen in public until the 1930s; but by then all Victorian painting was out of favour and Dadd regarded as a curiosity. By a quirk of fate, *The Fairy Feller* passed into the collection of the poet Siegfried Sassoon who donated it to the Tate Gallery in 1963 in memory of three brothers he had served with in the First World War, Julian, Edmund and Stephen Dadd – the great-nephews of Richard Dadd.

CHAPTER NINE

JOSEPH NOEL PATON RSA
1821-1901

Joseph Noel Paton, 'Puck and the Fairy'. *A small scene from 'A Midsummer Night's Dream', the subject which inspired Paton's two greatest pictures. This does not seem to be a specific incident in the play, but shows Puck lunging towards a beautiful, Pre-Raphaelite fairy who covers her nakedness with long blonde hair. The shell on her head suggests that she is a water sprite or sea nymph.*

Sir Joseph Noel Paton is chiefly remembered today as the Scottish Pre-Raphaelite, but he also painted some of the most remarkable fairy pictures. More than any of the other fairy painters, Paton combined incredible technical ability with a knowledge of folklore. An erudite and intellectual man, Paton studied Scottish folklore and Celtic legends, and put much of his knowledge into his paintings. Stylistically, his work is comparable to that of Maclise and Huskisson, but he outclassed both of them in his technique and the richness of his imagination. Paton and Dadd painted the same subjects, but Dadd's insanity sets him apart from his contemporaries; he belongs in a class of his own.

Paton was the son of a damask designer, and worked in Paisley designing textiles, before going to London to study at the Royal Academy Schools. Here he met the youthful prodigy Millais in 1843 and, had he stayed in London, he might have become a member of the Pre-Raphaelite Brotherhood. As it is, Paton, along with William Dyce, became one of the important Scottish followers of the Pre-Raphaelites, producing such masterpieces as *The Bluidie Tryst* and *Hesperus*.

Returning to Scotland, Paton turned to historical subjects, but in the late 1840s he produced two of the finest of Victorian pictures of 'A Midsummer Night's Dream'. The first, painted in 1847, was entitled *The Reconciliation of Oberon and Titania*, and it made his reputation. It was shown at the Royal Scottish Academy, and entered for the Westminster Hall Competitions, where it won a

JOSEPH NOEL PATON

Joseph Noel Paton, 'The Reconciliation of Oberon and Titania' (1847). *Paton painted 'The Reconciliation' in 1847, before completing 'The Quarrel' in 1849. Although the Pre-Raphaelite Brotherhood had not yet been formed, Paton's work anticipates their minutely detailed style. Both pictures contain large numbers of naked nymphs and amorous episodes, yet Paton was not criticised for this. As a technician, Paton is more skilled even than Maclise or Dadd.*

£300 prize. The critics were unanimous in praising what seemed an astonishing *tour de force* for such a young artist, then only twenty-six. 'The Times' critic thought that it surpassed 'every attempt we have seen at the illustration of the play'. Although the Pre-Raphaelite Brotherhood was not formed till 1848, Paton's two 'The Dream' pictures – *The Reconciliation* and the later *The Quarrel* – are in a way the first Pre-Raphaelite fairy pictures in which both the landscape settings and the figures are observed with the minutest fidelity.

The Reconciliation is conceived as a dream scene imagined by two sleeping lovers who are depicted as life size, Titania on the left, and Bottom in the centre. In the centre stand the partially naked figures of Oberon and Titania, who are slightly less than life size. In Act IV, Scene i, Titania has awoken from her dream, and is reconciled with Oberon:

    Titania: My Oberon! What visions have I have seen
              Me thought I was enamoured of an ass.
    Oberon: There lies your love.

Above the heads of Oberon and Titania is a ring of naked fairies circling, a device used by Maclise, Huskisson and Dadd. The rest of the picture is filled with a host of fairies, mostly naked female figures, and smaller goblins, elves, animals and other tiny figures. The presence of quite so many naked females generates a highly erotic charge, and it seems amazing that mid-Victorian prudery did not condemn Paton for this. In the cleft tree on the right is what appears to be a fairy bordello; by the tree to the left a naked nymph is carried off by a youth. Clearly such explicit scenes were pardonable in the fairy world, and were not therefore seen as a threat to public morals. Paton's figures owe a considerable debt to the work of William Etty, and even more to his follower, William

JOSEPH NOEL PATON

Edward Frost. Both Etty and Frost had been painting classical and allegorical subjects, involving large numbers of nude figures for years. Frost's pictures were always regarded as entirely proper, and one critic even complained that one of his female nudes looked as if 'she had been compressed by the stay'.

Encouraged by his success, Paton went to even more audacious lengths with his next fairy picture, *The Quarrel of Oberon and Titania*, completed in 1849. With this he went backwards in the play, to Act II, Scene i, where Oberon and Titania are quarrelling over the Indian changeling boy.

The scene is set, once again, in a dark wood, painted with a breathtaking accuracy equal to any Pre-Raphaelite landscape, particularly in the the gnarled old

trees, the flowers and leaves, and the lily pond in the foreground.

In the centre stand the same two figures of Oberon and Titania, with the Indian boy cowering behind Titania. Above her head a circle of nymphs forms a radiant halo, a novel touch and, to the left, another troupe of nymphs floats away, very similar in style to groups of female figures painted by Frost. The rest of the picture is a riot of naked fairies, both male and female, and the erotic temperature is raised even higher by the fact that numerous amorous incidents and fairy couplings are taking place. In particular on the right, under a statue of Pan with his pipes, naked couples are embracing and lolling on the ground in a highly

suggestive way. Amazingly, none of this attracted criticism; on the contrary, the picture was a great success, when exhibited at the Royal Scottish Academy in 1850. In addition to the naked fairies, Paton filled the picture with other strange figures of elves, goblins and imps, often involved in incidents with animals, particularly snails and moths. There are other small, grotesque figures here and there, possibly characters from Scottish folklore. The Rev. C.L. Dodgson, who had not yet made his name as Lewis Carroll, author of 'Alice's Adventures in Wonderland', saw Paton's picture in Edinburgh in 1857, and wrote in amazement, 'We counted one hundred and sixty-five fairies'.

Joseph Noel Paton, 'The Quarrel of Oberon and Titania' (1849). *Paton's great fairy pictures fulfil the Pre-Raphaelites ideal of painting nature with the greatest degree of accuracy and detail. Even if Paton had never seen a fairy, he certainly painted them as if he had. Lewis Carroll saw the picture in 1857, and counted 165 fairies, but neither he nor the critics remarked on the number of naked female fairies, nor their amorous couplings. Obviously such erotic scenes were thought permissible in the fairy world.*

It was not until 1867, that Paton produced his last and greatest fairy picture, *The Fairy Raid*. In the interim, he had painted many of his finest Pre-Raphaelite pictures, and his work had also become distinctly more moralistic in tone, as is shown by *The Pursuit of Pleasure* of 1855. This curious picture shows a procession of bacchanalian revellers, including a monk and a knight in armour, pursuing a nubile nymph with wings, long blonde tresses and come-hither eyes. Above hovers the shadowy figure of the avenging angel with a sword, making Paton's moral standpoint quite clear. The point would not have been lost on a Victorian audience which would certainly understand such a sermon in paint. The picture was engraved in 1855 (page 92) and doubtless proved a popular item in many a Victorian parlour. The Victorians rejected pleasure, but they did want to see what it looked like. In the same spirit, Frith painted several pictures on the theme of gambling, something equally abhorrent to the Victorians.

These changes are repeated in Paton's *The Fairy Raid*, for which the full title was *Carrying off the Changeling, Midsummer Eve* (pages 94 and 95). This time Paton has turned to Scottish folklore

After Joseph Noel Paton, 'The Pursuit of Pleasure' (1855, engraving). *The Victorians disapproved of pleasure, but did not mind their artists showing them what it looked like. Paton's column of pleasure-seekers, pursuing the coy figure of pleasure, is a fairy picture with a moral; the hovering angel of retribution above emphasising the message.*

for inspiration rather than Shakespeare. As a keen reader of Walter Scott, in particular his 'Minstrelsy of the Scottish Border', Paton turned to 'The Lady of the Lake' for Scott's account of a 'fairy rade' in the ballad 'Alice Brand':

> 'Tis merry, 'tis merry in Fairy-land,
> When fairy birds are singing,
> When the court doth ride by their monarch's side,
> With bit and bridle ringing.

A 'fairy rade', or a parade of fairies, was an ancient Scottish folk tale, handed down through centuries in old traditional ballads and songs. In combining this tale with the 'changeling' legend (another traditional belief that fairies could carry off a new-born child and substitute one of their own) Paton has cleverly brought two legends together.

Once again, as in the *Oberon and Titania* paintings, the picture is set at twilight in a dark wood through which winds the fairy procession, led by tiny mounted knights in armour. In the centre, the fairy queen, seated on a horse, holds the abducted baby. Around her are other mounted figures, and in the shadows other elves, gnomes and folkloric characters caper merrily.

Compared to the *Oberon and Titania* pictures, there is a distinct absence of naked fairies, and no sign of the fairy couplings in *The Quarrel*. Instead, a fairy knight impales a dragon on his lance to the right, bringing a chivalric tone to this fairyland. Beyond to the left are several standing stones; many of these stone circles still survive in western Scotland and the Hebrides, a link with those ancient Celtic beliefs in which Paton was so interested. Another Scottish legend relates that a visit to the stones on Midsummer Eve would propitiate the 'wee folk' and ensure good luck. Paton has thus brought together antiquarianism, folklore and chivalry in a typically mid-Victorian way, and one which was all part of the gradual process of cleaning up fairyland which took place during the Victorian period. In *The Fairy Raid* Paton has given us a new sanitised vision of fairyland, one acceptable to the Victorian middle classes and suitable for all the family. While the *The Fairy Raid* still harks back to the world of Maclise, Huskisson, Fitzgerald and Dadd, the darker, more shocking side of fairyland has been discreetly eliminated. We are on the way to Peter Pan and Wendy. Thereafter, Paton turned away from fairyland, concentrating increasingly on religious pictures for the last part of his long career. But he had created three of the greatest Victorian fairy pictures.

Paton also became involved in large Scottish monuments, such as the Stirling Wallace Memorial, and the Memorial of the War of Independence under Wallace and Bruce. The models for these can be seen in the painting by John Ballantyne of Noel Paton in his studio in 1867, one of a series of pictures of celebrated artists at work in their studios. Paton was appointed Her Majesty's Limner for Scotland and knighted in 1866.

Above and left: Details from Paton's great work 'The Fairy Raid.'

Overleaf: Joseph Noel Paton, 'The Fairy Raid' (1867). *The last of Paton's great fairy pictures completed in 1867, after six years' work. Paton was well versed in Scottish history and folklore, in which a 'fairy rade' is a parade or ride of fairies, of which numerous accounts in the Highlands were recorded. The fairy princess carries a changeling child on her horse, preceded by a band of fairy soldiers. Beyond is a ring of standing stones, a reminder of Druid ceremonies and ancient magic. The Scots visited these stones on Midsummer Eve to propitiate the fairy folk.*

JOSEPH NOEL PATON

JOSEPH NOEL PATON

JOSEPH NOEL PATON

Above and right: Joseph Noel Paton, 'Under the Sea I' *and* 'Under the Sea II'. *Fairies have always been associated with water, with rivers, lakes and the sea. Paton has here depicted two water nymphs, or naiads, a favourite subject for Victorian painters wishing to paint the female nude. On the right, the figure with the flying hair, conversing with the fish, is a particularly remarkable, proto-Symbolist, image.*

CHAPTER TEN

JOHN ANSTER FITZGERALD
1832-1906

John Anster Fitzgerald, 'The Artist's Dream' (1857). *Fitzgerald's pictures of sleeping figures and their dreams are his most remarkable contribution to fairy painting. Here the artist, perhaps Fitzgerald himself, has fallen asleep in his chair. In his dream he sees himself painting at an easel; the beautiful model turns to look at him. All around hover fantastic goblins, one offering a goblet, one of many references in Fitzgerald's work to opiates and drugs.*

With 'Fairy Fitzgerald' we come to the one Victorian artist to devote most of his career to painting fairies. After his death in 1906, Aaron Watson, writing in 'The Savage Club' (1907), described him as 'an artist who will probably be more appreciated in time to come than he is in his own life time', a prediction that has indeed come true. Fitzgerald is now appreciated more than ever before, and recognised as the most dedicated, and in many ways the most fascinating, of the fairy painters.

What makes Fitzgerald's pictures different from those of the fairy painters before him is that he did not rely on literary inspiration. Fitzgerald's fairy world is not based on 'A Midsummer Night's Dream' or 'The Tempest', although he did paint these subjects occasionally (pages 44 and 45). It is a world of dreams, of nightmares, of the imagination, a world entirely populated by creatures of his own creative power. Like Maclise, Huskisson or Noel Paton, Fitzgerald does combine reality with fantasy, but he does so in a quite unique and personal way. As a result his pictures are more compellingly real and convincing than most other fairy pictures. More than any of his contemporaries, Fitzgerald succeeds in depicting on canvas the deeper and darker recesses of the Victorian subconscious.

Fitzgerald's life and career were in most respects typical of a Victorian artist. Born in 1832, his life spans the whole of Queen Victoria's reign, and he died in the first decade of the twentieth century. His ancestry was Irish. His grandfather was an Irish soldier-adventurer, and his father, William Fitzgerald, an actor, now

JOHN ANSTER FITZGERALD

JOHN ANSTER FITZGERALD

John Anster Fitzgerald, 'Fairies attacking a Bat'. *Bats, like fairies, are creatures of the night, and here fairies are tormenting a bat, silhouetted against the moon. Several fairies are goading the bat with thorns; more ghostly, semi-transparent figures fly in from the left.*

only remembered in the mocking lines of Byron's 'English Bards and Scotch Reviewers':

> Let hoarse Fitzgerald bawl
> His creaking couplets in a tavern hall.

John Anster was William's third son. Nothing is known of his artistic training, but by the 1840s he was exhibiting at the Royal Academy, the British Institution, and the Royal Society of British Artists. He continued to exhibit for the next fifty years (such productivity was not unusual in the Victorian age, the animal painter Thomas Sidney Cooper exhibited at the Royal Academy for sixty-three years without a break; it is still a record). Fitzgerald did not only paint fairy subjects – he also painted historical and other figurative subjects, and was also an illustrator, mostly for 'The Illustrated London News'. He is also known to have painted portraits, and the occasional nude. But his other pictures are conventional and run-of-the-mill; it was his fairy pictures that ignited his imaginative abilities, and it for these that he is now remembered. Fitzgerald also worked in watercolour, and used watercolour for a number of his fairy pictures.

All Fitzgerald's fairy pictures date from the 1850s and 1860s, and as yet no later works have come to light. This is surprising, because he was known as 'Fairy Fitzgerald' to the end of his career. Possibly he was forced to turn to other work from the 1870s onwards, as his type of fairy picture went out of fashion. His reputation now rests on a small group of 'dream' pictures of sleeping figures, all dating from the 1850s, and his fairy pictures and watercolours, which mostly date from the late 1850s and 1860s.

The connection between fairy painting and the theatre has already been pointed out. In Fitzgerald's case, we know of his theatrical connections, not only through his actor father, but also through his drawings for 'The Illustrated London News', which are mostly pantomime scenes, such as his *Fairyland* of 1867. In this drawing Fitzgerald created a highly stagey scene, but elaborated it with fantastical creatures and birds from his own imagination, and set it among holly leaves, to give it a Christmas flavour. A fairy feast of fruit is set upon a toadstool; a dwarfish master of ceremonies with a large belly and an astonishing crown directs an elf to struggle forward carrying a cherry. All around are other figures and weird beasts, more wispily sketched in, a common technique with Fitzgerald. The fairy queen

John Anster Fitzgerald, 'The Pond Fairies'. *Fitzgerald worked in watercolour as well as oil. In watercolour, his fairies are even more transparent and wispy, almost evanescent, as if they might at any moment disappear. Here fairies are playing among reeds and bulrushes.*

JOHN ANSTER FITZGERALD

holds a dove, a symbol of peace, in her lap, as a grinning and grotesque waiter hands round some fiendish brew in bowls. Other revellers in extravagant costumes of leaves and wings hover in the foreground. The drawing has all the trappings of a Victorian pantomime scene, yet transmuted by Fitzgerald into something genuinely magical and convincing. Fitzgerald's use of light in his pictures is also distinctly theatrical. Although his subjects are usually nocturnal, the central figures are usually lit by an intensely bright, dazzling light, reminiscent of the gaslight or limelight used in the Victorian theatre. His colours can also be garish; he favoured a distinct range of reds, oranges, blues and purples, which may also reflect the influence of pantomime.

Fitzgerald's most remarkable works are a small group of pictures of dreaming figures. The first, dated 1857, is entitled *The Artist's Dream* (page 99), and shows an artist, no doubt Fitzgerald himself, who has fallen asleep in his chair. In the background is a vision of the artist at his easel painting a beautiful fairy with a convolvulus flower over her head. A fiendish goblin mockingly holds a wreath of flowers over the artist's head. The fairy model, who looks like La Sylphide, or a

John Anster Fitzgerald, 'The Enchanted Forest'. *The fairies' relationship with the animal kingdom is a frequent subject in fairy painting, and one much explored by Fitzgerald. Here a herd of deer nervously approach a group of amazingly weird fairies and goblins, one resembling a flying fish.*

figure from a romantic ballet, turns her head to look at the sleeping artist. Around his chair hover various grotesque goblins, some sketched in lightly using grey and transparent colours, some brightly coloured. One of the goblins on the left holds up a crystal goblet. This is one of several references in Fitzgerald's works to sleeping draughts, suggesting that it is drugs or opiates that have induced this strange dream. We do not know where Fitzgerald drew inspiration for the many grotesque and fantastical creatures in his paintings, though it seems most likely that he found them in Flemish paintings, particularly the work of Hieronymus Bosch and Pieter Brueghel the Elder.

Fitzgerald's other 'dream' pictures are all of sleeping girls. The most extraordinary of them is *The Nightmare*, a watercolour of about 1857–8. A pretty

John Anster Fitzgerald, 'Robin defending his Nest' (circa 1858–60). *Fitzgerald painted a number of pictures featuring Robin Redbreast. Here Robin defends his nest against fairies, one wielding a thorn. The violation of birds' nests and eggs was a frequent theme of fairy painting, and also features in the pictures of Hieronymus Bosch. Fitzgerald must also have been familiar with the birds' nests watercolours of W. H. Hunt.*

JOHN ANSTER FITZGERALD

John Anster Fitzgerald, 'The Captive Dreamer' (1856). *Unlike Fitzgerald's other 'dream' paintings, this one is set in a landscape. The girl lies asleep on the branch of a tree, which looks like a sleeping dragon. One of her wrists is chained to a tree. To the right fairies lead a knight in armour towards her, perhaps he is her rescuer.*

young girl writhes on her bed, in the grip of a nightmare. In the background she appears in three dream sequences. In the first, she holds hands with a lover by the light of a full moon; next, she is waylaid by two masked men in seventeenth century costume carrying drawn swords; finally, a man kneels beside her while a man and woman flee away. It is a dream of love and betrayal, and the young girl lies on her bed surrounded by mocking fiends, one of whom bows obsequiously to her. In this picture, Fitzgerald drops the heaviest hints that the girl's dreams are drug-induced. Not only are there coloured medicine bottles by the bed, but two of the goblins are holding trays of glasses, and another a bowl from which steam rises. One can only speculate what these fiendish potions might be, but they are clearly meant to imply that they are the cause of the girl's nightmares. The point is emphasised by her change of costume. In the dream scenes she is wearing white robes and a wreath of white flowers. On the bed she wears a Turkish-style embroidered jacket and coloured sash, while a white wreath has fallen from her head. The coloured sash spills over the bed and down the side, and looks uncannily like blood. The table beside the bed is also Middle-Eastern in style. The use of drugs and opiates was unrestricted in Victorian times, and Fitzgerald is seeming to suggest that the goblins are luring her to an overdose, or even to take poison. The artist Rossetti was addicted to chloral, and his wife, Elizabeth Siddal, died from an overdose of laudanum, so there was no lack of parallels in real life for Fitzgerald to follow. But never again was he to refer quite so openly to drugs.

Two other 'dream' pictures date from around 1858 and are both entitled *The Stuff that Dreams are made of*. Both show sleeping girls surrounded by dream scenes and grotesque creatures, but in both the references to narcotics have been

John Anster Fitzgerald, 'The Stuff that Dreams are made of' (circa 1858). *One of the group of pictures by Fitzgerald of sleeping girls. This girl seems to be having pleasant dreams, not nightmares. In the background are a pair of lovers, the man in seventeenth century dress. Around the bed hover goblins and monsters, one to the left carries a tray of glasses.*

John Anster Fitzgerald, 'The Fledgling'. *Another bird subject, this time a fat and greedy fledgling. The fairies fly in with a constant supply of fruit and berries to assuage his appetite. Two fairies on the right are carrying in a moth; another brings an acorn cup bowl. As always, Fitzgerald's girl fairies wear fantastical headgear and crowns.*

definitely toned down. Both girls have wreaths of flowers in their hair; one wears a fur-lined jacket, the other a richly embroidered jacket with a sash which look somewhat exotic and oriental. In the background of both pictures are dream loves scenes in which the girl appears together with a lover in historical costume, with bunches of mistletoe over their heads. Hovering around both girls are the usual assortment of fiends and goblins, often with grotesque heads and bodies, but stick-like arms and legs. Some are carrying glasses or drinking from them, but there is much less emphasis on this aspect than in *The Nightmare*. In both pictures the goblins are generally merry and not as menacing as those in *The Nightmare*. Many of them play musical instruments; on a chair by the bed one is using a hat-box as a drum. Both girls seem to be sleeping peacefully, unlike the tortured figure of the girl in the grip of a nightmare. Fitzgerald seems to have painted these pictures for public exhibition, reducing the references to drugs to the minimum so as not to offend or alarm potential buyers. But taken as a group, Fitzgerald's 'dream' pictures are among the most fascinating of Victorian fairy paintings, making him the only real successor to Fuseli.

Fitzgerald's other fairy pictures are similarly highly individual and imaginative. Unlike the work of Dadd, Maclise and Noel Paton, they are based not on literary

JOHN ANSTER FITZGERALD

sources but on fairy folklore and Fitzgerald's own imagination. These pictures are usually small, no more than ten or twelve inches across, but brightly coloured, and packed with figures and incidents. Certain themes tend to recur. One is the 'fairy banquet'. There are many accounts in folklore of sightings of fairies banqueting, or of humans eating fairy food, often with ill effects. In Fitzgerald's pictures, the fairy queen usually sits at a toadstool laden with elaborate bowls of fruit. Round the toadstool table the fairies congregate, usually with wings and highly ornamental flower head-dresses. They are usually pretty, with girlish smiling faces. Around them hover the usual assortment of grotesque hobgoblins and weird creatures,

John Anster Fitzgerald, 'The Fairies' Banquet' (1859). *Among the other delicacies described by Robert Herrick in his poem 'Oberon's Feast' (see page 32) are:*

'*Beards of mice, a Newt's stewed thigh
A bloated earwig, and a Flie*'.

John Anster Fitzgerald, 'The Fairies' Barque' (1860). *The fairy's barque is a waterlily, probably inspired by the publicity surrounding the successful cultivation of the giant waterlily,* Victoria regia. *This was one of the few pictures exhibited by Fitzgerald; at the British Institution in 1860, when it was priced at £35. As it was an exhibited picture, Fitzgerald has excluded any hints of cruelty.*

who grin fiendishly and hand out food and drink. The setting is a background of leaves and flowers, usually convolvulus, symbolic of night and sleep. A similar formula is followed in *The Fairies' Barque*; here the fairy queen sits in a barque fashioned from a waterlily, while her attendants row with bulrushes for oars. The giant water lily *Victoria regia* had first been grown in England by Joseph Paxton at Chatsworth, and many fairy painters and illustrators featured them in their pictures.

Another recurring theme in Fitzgerald's painting is a birds' nest with eggs. This was a subject first popularised by the watercolourist William Henry Hunt, known as 'Birds' Nest Hunt' whose pictures combine minute observation,

JOHN ANSTER FITZGERALD

sentiment and cruelty giving them a typically Victorian *frisson*. Fitzgerald gives the birds' nest a new twist by introducing it in to fairyland. The eggs are usually being attacked by goblins and fairies and defended by birds. The idea of violating birds' eggs also features in the work of Hieronymus Bosch, as does the idea of grotesque creatures emerging from eggs, which was also used by Fitzgerald. In one of his pictures, Fitzgerald shows three fairies in a birds' nest. This picture is in one of the celebrated 'twiggy' frames used by Fitzgerald. Made of gilded wood the shape of interlacing twigs, these are very delicate and, only one or two have survived (see page 192).

John Anster Fitzgerald, 'Who killed Cock Robin?' *One of several versions Fitzgerald painted of this subject. In country folklore, it was always thought unlucky either to keep or kill a robin. Traditionally, robins were friendly to humans, and were thought to cover up or bury the bodies of people who died in the woods.*

JOHN ANSTER FITZGERALD

John Anster Fitzgerald, 'The Fairy's Funeral' (1864). *Folklore is full of fairy funerals, and accounts gleaned from oral tradition were published by nineteenth century antiquarians, such as Thomas Crofton Croker and Thomas Keightley. William Blake witnessed a fairy burial in his own garden. For once, Fitzgerald has invested this fairy scene with an atmosphere of solemnity.*

In many of his birds' nest pictures, Fitzgerald featured Robin Redbreast, best-loved of British birds. Sometimes Robin is defending his nest against fairies attacking with sharp thorns. In another picture, robin is held captive, and drawn by fairy reins made of flowers. In folklore, it was very unlucky to kill or capture a robin, as robins were said to bury people who died or were murdered in the woods by covering their bodies with leaves. This meant that robins and fairies were often in conflict, and this is the theme of most of Fitzgerald's *Cock Robin* pictures. The death and burial of Cock Robin is another favourite theme, usually titled after the nursery rhyme, 'Who killed Cock Robin?'

Other creatures featured by Fitzgerald were white mice, usually being chased,

JOHN ANSTER FITZGERALD

goaded or tormented by fairies and goblins, in a cheerful but not too overtly sadistic way. There is however an underlying current of cruelty in these pictures, as there is in the Cock Robin pictures.

Sightings of fairy funerals were one of the most common incidents in folklore and were recorded in all the Victorian anthologies. Inevitably, Fitzgerald painted fairy funerals, and exhibited one at the British Institution in 1864.

Fitzgerald made frequent use of watercolour. In this medium he used pale, evanescent colours, and was able to achieve ghostly effects quite different in feeling from his oils. In one of these, a troupe of sylph-like fairies in elaborate

John Anster Fitzgerald, 'The Fairy Falconer'. *A fairy rests on a cornstalk, holding a falcon in its lap, suggesting the falcon is being used to catch birds. Two other fairy huntsmen stand holding thorns. Fairies often tease, chase or even hurt animals in Fitzgerald's pictures.*

JOHN ANSTER FITZGERALD

Above: Joseph Oppenheim, 'Old J.A. Fitzgerald' (1903). *A portrait of 'Fairy Fitzgerald', the longest-lived and most productive of Victorian fairy painters.*

Right: John Anster Fitzgerald, 'The Old Hall, Fairies by Moonlight'. *Fairies dance around a haunted-looking house, by the light of the moon. Some of Fitzgerald's watercolours are painted in this loose, impressionistic style, but the sheer exuberance and range of his imagination marks him out as one of the great fairy painters.*

Far right: John Anster Fitzgerald, 'Christmas Eve'. *Another watercolour, this time showing fairies as winter creatures, as if made of ice, and taking away the toys which have been left down the chimney.*

costumes look through a Gothic arch. The exact title or theme is unknown, but it could be a scene from ballet, like so many fairy pictures.

Very little is known of Fitzgerald's career after 1870, yet he continued working for another thirty years. His oil sketch *The Pipe Dream*, which dates from about 1870, contains more tantalising references to opium-smoking and dreams. At the Savage Club, Fitzgerald was known for his impersonations of famous actors like Kemble, Kean and Macready, usually delivered in an Irish brogue, like his father's poetry. Long after Fitzgerald's death, Harry Furniss wrote affectionately about him in 'My Bohemian Days' (1919):

> He was a picturesque old chap, imbued…with the traditions of the transportine drama [i.e. that of the Old Vic]…He had a mobile face, a twinkling eye, and his hair was long, thick and thrown back from his face… He was known as 'Fairy Fitzgerald' from the fact that his work, both colour and black-and-white, was devoted to fairy scenes, in fact his life was one long Midsummer Night's Dream.

JOHN ANSTER FITZGERALD

CHAPTER ELEVEN

RICHARD DOYLE
1824-1883

& CHARLES ALTAMONT DOYLE 1832-1893

Richard Doyle, 'Temptation'. *Doyle's fairy pictures have a gentle humour and fantasy that is utterly delightful, and quite distinctively his own. His work lacks the darker vein of cruelty, and nightmares, that pervade the work of Fitzgerald, and he was the perfect illustrator of children's books. Doyle's work, unlike that of Fitzgerald and the earlier Victorian fairy painters, was suitable for all the family. The fairy here tempting an owl is typical of Doyle's gentler approach.*

One of the best-loved of the Victorian fairy painters, both as an artist and a personality, was 'Dickie' Doyle. A man of endearing charm, he was a friend to many of the great and good of the Victorian art world. Holman Hunt wrote that Doyle was 'unique and delightful…a man overflowing with strange stories, but never with a word of uncharitableness'.

Doyle was born in to an artistic family. The second son of the caricaturist John Doyle (1797–1868), he showed artistic talent at a young age and joined the staff of 'Punch', where he designed the original cover. It was while on 'Punch' that he developed his ability to depict large crowds of small figures. He remained on the magazine until 1850, and thereafter devoted himself mainly to illustration, both of fairy books and contemporary subjects.

Nearly all Doyle's work was in watercolour, a medium in which he achieved considerable mastery. This, combined with his technique of filling the composition with large numbers of small figures, is shown in his watercolour *The Enchanted Fairy Tree*, dated 1845. This was one of his very few pictures to be exhibited at the Royal Academy. The full title is *The Enchanted Fairy Tree, or A Fantasy based on The Tempest*, but Doyle has not tried to depict any particular incident. To one side, a wizard with a beard, probably Prospero, remonstrates with his stick towards a multitude of small figures in the two palm trees, one of whom may be Ariel. The rest of the picture is full of tiny figures, mostly human, and humorous incidents, done in much the same way as Doyle's illustrations for

114

RICHARD DOYLE

Richard Doyle, watercolour vignettes and illustrations from 'In Fairyland'.
Above: 'An Intruder'.
Right: 'Reposing'.
Below: 'Fairy Child's Play'.
Far right above: 'The Triumphal March of the Elf King'.
Far right below: 'Courtship cut short'.

'Punch'. The humour is gentle, not threatening; there are no fiendish goblins or weird beasts as in Fitzgerald's work. This light-hearted atmosphere was to be characteristic of Doyle. He showed a similar aptitude for humour and fantasy in his large watercolour of *The Fairy Tree*. This also shows a large number of small figures and animals on the branches of a tree. Again, the figures are mostly human, but Doyle's inventiveness in creating different characters and incidents is extraordinary. Almost every single figure is a brilliant caricature or comic distortion. Doyle's vision of the fairy world was very much that of a 'Punch' cartoonist. It is the world of Dickens in miniature, rather than the fairy world of Fitzgerald or Noel Paton.

Doyle was at heart an illustrator, and he belongs more to the world of children's books than to that of fairy painters. It was as an illustrator that he made his name. In 1866, together with the dramatist and theatrical producer James Robinson Planché (1796–1880), he published 'An Old Fairy Tale told Anew'. A re-telling of 'The Sleeping Beauty', this was illustrated with eighteen black and white woodcuts, printed and published by the Dalziel Brothers. Doyle also illustrated Ruskin's only venture into fairyland, 'The King of the Golden River', and Thackeray's 'The Newcomes'. Thus he was used to illustrating the real world and the fairy world, and used the same style and technique for both.

His finest works, now regarded as his masterpiece, were his coloured illustrations for William Allingham's 'In Fairyland, or Pictures from the Elf World' (1869–70). This was a colour print book, and Doyle provided the printers, Edmund Evans, with thirty-six watercolour illustrations painted over the proof impressions. The quality and size of the resulting colour plates were exceptional for that date; they also show Doyle's style at its wittiest, most fanciful and

RICHARD DOYLE

inventive. Every plate is a delight: one shows a musical elf on a toadstool teaching a chorus of birds to sing; in another, the fairy queen takes an aerial drive on a flower drawn by butterflies (both overleaf). In *The Triumphal March of the Elf King*, a procession of elves play with snails, birds, butterflies and mice. In these plates, Doyle has allowed his fantasy full rein, and the results are some of the most charming and humorous of Victorian fairy images.

Doyle's style was imitated by many other illustrators of children's books, right up to the end of the nineteenth century and beyond. He was part of the late Victorian tendency to put the fairy world in the nursery, to reduce it to something delightful and harmless, and suitable for children. In Doyle's work, there is none of the dark side of fairyland, that we find in the work of Dadd, Maclise, Noel Paton or Fitzgerald.

Much the same could be said of Doyle's many other watercolours of fairies in landscapes. Most of

RICHARD DOYLE

Richard Doyle, watercolour vignettes and illustrations from 'In Fairyland'.
Above: 'The Tournament'.
Below: 'Rehearsal in Elfland – musical Elf teaching the young Birds to sing'.

these show elves and pixies dancing around trees, among toadstools, or under bracken. The landscape, which dominates the composition in the majority of these watercolours is always beautifully and naturalistically observed. Doyle makes one feel that fairies are completely part of the landscape, as in *Under the Dock Leaves* of 1878, now in the British Museum, so well has he blended the figures in to the background.

Doyle's landscape style is similar in feeling to that of the so-called 'Idyllists', a group of watercolourists centred around Fred Walker, and including John William North, George John Pinwell and Robert Walker MacBeth. Their aim was to move landscape away from the total realism of the Pre-Raphaelites, towards a more imaginative and poetic approach. Doyle was one of the very few artists who could successfully combine this approach with the world of fairyland.

Like many illustrators, Doyle longed for acceptance in the higher world of painting, and to this end he painted landscapes in oil, and sent them to the Royal Academy. They were not a success, for his real talents undoubtedly lay in the world of illustration. A successful show of his drawings and watercolours was held at the Grosvenor Gallery in 1881, but in spite of this Doyle died a disappointed man, on the steps of that most Victorian of institutions, the Athenaeum Club.

His entry in the 'Dictionary of National Biography' described him as, 'a singularly sweet and noble type of English gentleman…an artist of "most excellent fancy" – the kindliest of pictorial satirists, the most sportive and frolicsome of designers, the most graceful and sympathetic of fairyland. In Oberon's Court he would at once have been appointed sergeant-painter'.

Above: 'The Fairy Queen Takes an airy Drive'.
Below: 'Teasing a Butterfly'.

CHARLES ALTAMONT DOYLE

Like his older brother Richard, Charles Altamont Doyle was also a watercolourist and illustrator. But by contrast, with Charles we are back in the world of insanity and nightmares, the world of Fuseli and Dadd. The younger Doyle's career started promisingly. He joined the Edinburgh Office of Works at the age of nineteen and exhibited both watercolour and pen and ink studies at the Royal Scottish Academy. He illustrated a number of books, including 'Pilgrim's Progress' and 'London Society'. However, by the 1880s, his health began to break down, and he was admitted to the Montrose Royal Lunatic Asylum, suffering from alcoholism and epilepsy. He ironically referred to the asylum as 'Sunnyside'.

Charles Doyle's work is evidence of his split personality. Some of his fairy and fantasy subjects are highly colourful and inventive, like those of his elder brother,

Charles Altamont Doyle, 'Hearts are Trumps'. *A courting couple play cards in a landscape while fairies peep over their shoulders, and a dog looks on. The surreal atmosphere and slightly weird subject are both typical of Charles Doyle.*

and do include fairies. They have similar titles, such as *The Fairy Queen, A Procession* (overleaf), or *A Moon Fantasy*, which is equal in inventiveness to Richard.

But Charle's Doyle's later works, such as his *Self-Portrait, a Medidation*, strike an altogether more sinister note. Here the artist sits at his table, in his library, surrounded by flying figures and goblins. The atmosphere is much more hallucinatory and threatening. These later watercolours are generally done in a narrow range of grey and blue colours, unlike his more colourful fairy subjects. Charles's interest in dreams and the occult was inherited by his son, Sir Arthur Conan Doyle, the creator of Sherlock Holmes, who wrote the defence of the Cottingley fairies (see page 41).

Charles Altamont Doyle, 'A Dance around the Moon'. *Doyle's fairies are a collection of weird and grotesque people, rather than genuine fairies. In this respect, Doyle's work is similar to that of Dadd; insanity undoubtedly gave an edge to both men's work, a fact which sets them apart from other fairy painters.*

Top: Charles Altamont Doyle, 'The Fairy Queen, A Procession' (1882). *Similar in style to Richard Doyle's fairy processions, but the figures are mostly strange and weird grown-ups rather than fairies. Charles Doyle's work is much closer in spirit to that of Dadd, who like him, ended his life in a mental institution.*

Above: Charles Altamont Doyle, 'The Dragon Chariot'. *At its best, Charles Doyle's work has an exuberant fantasy unique among fairy painters.*

Above: Charles Altamont Doyle, 'The Fairy Picnic' (1882). *Charles Doyle's work has at times an altogether more fantastical and nightmarish quality that that of his brother. His interest in the spirit world was inherited by his son, Sir Arthur Conan Doyle, creator of Sherlock Holmes.*

CHAPTER TWELVE

Lesser Fairy Painters

John George Naish, 'Elves and Fairies: A Midsummer Night's Dream' (1856) *Fairies with butterfly wings play among flowers, one rides a moth, and others attack a caterpillar. The flowers are not those that decorate Titania's bower, as described by Shakespeare, but Victorian favourites – nasturtiums, geraniums and fuschias. Naish's work has a brilliant Pre-Raphaelite quality, similar to that of Huskisson and Paton. It is a pity he did not paint more fairy subjects.*

During the 1850s and 1860s the vogue for fairy painting led several other artists to try their hand at the subject. Some only painted one or two fairy pictures; others painted a handful, and then moved on to other subjects. In every age, there are artists prepared to trim their sails to the latest artistic breeze.

One such was John George Naish (1824–1905). During the 1850s he painted fairy and mythological subjects, including *Titania* in 1850. His best-known work is the remarkable *Elves and Fairies: A Midsummer Night's Dream* of 1856, which he exhibited at the British Institution. It shows fairies disporting among geraniums, fuchsias and nasturtiums, all popular Victorian favourites. A small fairy rides a moth while others attack a caterpillar. It is one of the most brilliant Victorian fairy pictures involving flowers. In the 1860s Naish moved to Ilfracombe in Devon, and for the rest of his career painted landscapes.

Naish's pictures usually contain a large number of pretty, naked female fairies, such as might well have excited the Victorian male viewer, examining them with his eye-glass. Another specialist in this area was John Simmons (1823–76), a little-known Bristol portrait painter and watercolourist. During the 1850s and 1860s he painted a number of scenes from 'A Midsummer Night's Dream', usually involving very pretty female nudes with wings. Reflecting his training as a miniaturist, Simmons' watercolours are executed with an astonishing clarity, high level of detail and smoothness of finish, as if painted on glass. As a result, they are distinctly titillating, but in a highly mid-Victorian way. This is where Victorian

LESSER FAIRY PAINTERS

Above: John George Naish, 'Moon Fairies II' (1853). *Fairies are often shown riding on birds but here one is shown is flying on a moth. Fairies are also shown flying or riding on the backs of other animals, particularly by Richard Doyle.*

Right: John Simmons, 'The Honey Bee steals from the Bumble Bees'. *Simmons' fairy watercolours invariably involve beautiful naked female fairies, reminding us that such a normally taboo subject was permissible in the fairy world.*

fairy painting comes dangerously close to 'Playboy Magazine'. The *poses plastiques* of Simmons' fairy queens are the bunny girls of the Victorian era.

Another painter of fairy nudes was Thomas Heatherley (circa 1824–1913), founder of the famous art school that bears his name, and survives today. Many famous Victorian artists studied at Heatherley's, including Rossetti, Burne-Jones, Arthur Hughes and Walter Crane. Heatherley did not often exhibit his own work, but he painted the occasional fairy picture, such as his *Fairy Seated on a Mushroom* of about 1860 (page 130). This shows a back view of a naked fairy with long red hair, and other naked fairies hovering in the sky. The other grotesque figures are reminiscent of similar goblins in the work of Dadd and Fitzgerald.

After 1870, the vogue for fairy painting declined, and thereafter fairies only occasionally crop up, usually in the work of late romantic artists who also painted mythological, literary or fantasy subjects. One surprising late contributor to the fairy vogue was the Leeds painter of moonlight scenes, Atkinson Grimshaw

John Simmons. 'A Fairy among Convolvulus'. *This Victorian Venus – a typical Simmons pin-up – reposes among convolvulus. Such highly erotic images were possible for fairy painters, but would otherwise be inadmissible in the mid-Victorian art world.*

(1836–93). Although predominantly a painter of landscapes, town scenes, and docks, Grimshaw began to paint romantic, figurative subjects in the 1870s, such as his celebrated *Elaine* of 1877. He also painted a number of Tissot-like aesthetic interiors, usually painted in his own house, using his wife as model. The family's German governess was said to have modelled for his first nude, entitled *Dame Autumn hath a Mournful Face* (1871). This shows a lightly draped nude figure, floating in a brilliant nimbus of light, set against a dark and atmospheric landscape background. Grimshaw used the same technique with his only fairy picture, *Iris*, of which he painted two versions. This too shows a nude female figure hovering

LESSER FAIRY PAINTERS

above a lake, her face and figure enveloped in a glowing halo of light which is reflected on her iridescent wings (page 132). The background is a typical Grimshaw landscape, brown and autumnal, with a web of criss-crossing trees; the foreground is lined with withered grasses and rushes along the edge of the water. It is a remarkably effective and haunting fairy image, and one can only wish Grimshaw had painted more of these, and fewer versions of Liverpool docks. The few other nudes he painted in this way were all of classical subjects, such as *Diana the Huntress* and *Ariadne on Naxos*.

Edward Robert Hughes, RWS (1851–1914), was a nephew of the artist Arthur Hughes, and therefore grew up in Pre-Raphaelite circles. In particular, Hughes was friendly with Holman Hunt, and worked as his studio assistant when Hunt was growing old and blind. Like Burne-Jones, Hughes worked mainly in

John Simmons, 'The Evening Star'. *Another Victorian Venus reposes among roses and honeysuckle. Simmons' work is in general more concerned with ideal female beauty than with fairies. This however, was one of the functions of Victorian fairy painting.*

LESSER FAIRY PAINTERS

Thomas Heatherley. 'Fairy seated on a Mushroom' (circa 1860). *Heatherley is now chiefly remembered as a teacher, and founder of Heatherley's Academy. He painted one or two genre and historical pictures, and a small number of fairy pictures. Here a beautiful nymph with long red hair, her back view reminiscent of Ingres, sits on a mushroom – a frequent image in fairy paintings, suggestive of sex and hallucinatory dreams.*

watercolour or gouache. His subjects are the usual late romantic mixture of literary, mythological, and pure fantasy. His technique was meticulous, yet tinged with a feeling of mystery and poetry, and that wistfulness of mood so typical of the turn of the century. His only pure fairy subject was *Midsummer Eve* (page 133), showing a girl, or perhaps a wood-nymph, standing in the middle of a ring of fairies in a dark wood. This magical atmosphere is typical of Hughes, whatever subject he was painting. Above all, he was an artist trying to convey a mood, rather than depict a particular narrative.

Also connected with the Pre-Raphaelites, and also a watercolourist, was Eleanor Fortescue-Brickdale (1872–1945). She was the first woman to be elected to the Royal Institute of Oil Painters and taught at her friend Byam Shaw's Art School in Kensington. She worked both in oil and in gouache, in a highly-wrought and elaborate style, similar to both Byam Shaw and E.R. Hughes. She was also a prolific illustrator, but painted only a few specifically fairy subjects. The most outstanding one is *The Lover's World* of 1905 (page 136). Like Hughes' *Midsummer Eve*, this shows the single figure of a girl in a wood, surrounded by fairies, flowers and birds. But the mood is completely different, and the colours considerably stronger and brighter. The symbolism is more obvious, with the rainbow, the dove and the owls. The fairies gambol in the flowers, and also hold a bridal wreath over the girl's head, hinting at her future nuptials. This lush version of the fairy world is typical of the new mood of the Edwardian period: fairies are sweet, pretty and charming, and no longer threatening to humans; they have become merely decorative, and something for the children. This was the age of 'Peter Pan', first produced in 1904, the year before Fortescue-Brickdale's *Lover's World*.

Several other lady artists who painted fairies deserve mention. Etheline E. Dell (fl.1885–91) painted a few watercolours of fairies, mostly based on 'A Midsummer Night's Dream' (pages 138 and 139). They are usually small, but intensely coloured, and full of figures. Adelaide and Florence Claxton, the daughters of an artist, were both accomplished watercolourists in the 1870s and 1880s. Adelaide (fl.1859–79) made something of a speciality of 'ghost' subjects,

LESSER FAIRY PAINTERS

usually showing a girl asleep, or reading a book, surrounded by apparitions and fairy-like figures flying around. Although not specifically fairy subjects, these watercolours reveal the continuing Victorian fascination with the spirit world, manifested in the current vogue for séances and mediums.

Both Sophie Anderson (1823–1903) and Laura Gwenllian James (exh. 1897–1907) painted delightful fairy pictures, and one can only wish they had painted more. Sophie Anderson was well-known as a painter of girls, and sometimes depicted them as fairies (page 141). Laura James, wife of Walter James, Lord Northbourne, a talented landscape painter, was herself a talented amateur (page 140). Amateurs with above-average talent were common in the upper reaches of society in Victorian times. Some, like George Howard and Lady Waterford, were professionals, but prevented by their position from practising as such.

Frederick George Cotman (1850–1920), nephew of John Sell Cotman, was one of an artistic dynasty. He was primarily a landscapist, but occasionally painted figurative subjects of fairy apparitions appearing to a young girl (page 155).

Thomas Heatherley, 'Fairies among Mushrooms' (circa 1860). *A beautiful naked female fairy sleeps on a mushroom, while another fairy watches over her. In front, fairies attack a snail, while others dance on the edge of a mushroom. Like Simmons, Heatherley's fairy pictures usually involve female nudes.*

LESSER FAIRY PAINTERS

Above: Atkinson Grimshaw, 'Iris, Spirit of the Rainbow' (1876). Iris, the messenger of the gods, was sent to wither flowers in the autumn, but she stopped to admire the waterlilies, and as a punishment was turned in to a rainbow. Grimshaw's eerily-lit figure, with its golden aura, reflects the growing Victorian interest in spiritualism and the supernatural. Another version of this picture, painted in 1886, is in Leeds City Art Gallery.

Right: Edward Robert Hughes. 'Midsummer Eve'. Hughes had impeccable Pre-Raphaelite credentials; he was a nephew of Arthur Hughes and assistant to William Holman Hunt. Like Burne-Jones, he worked mainly in watercolour and gouache, and was also a beautiful draughtsman. His subjects, like most of the late Romantics, were mainly literary and mythological; only occasionally did he paint a fairy subject such as this.

Right: Edward Robert Hughes, 'Twilight Fantasies'. Like many of Hughes' pictures, this is a fantasy, aimed at creating a mood, rather than any specific subject. The shepherdess plays her pipe at twilight, conjuring up a cavalcade of fairy angels, who flit through the woods playing musical instruments.

Overleaf left: Eleanor Fortescue-Brickdale, 'The Lover's World' (1905). Many of the later Romantics painted woodland scenes such as this, in which a single figure is surrounded by a fairy horde, here about to crown the Pre-Raphaelite maiden in her medieval dress with a wreath of flowers. Fortescue-Brickdale has deliberately introduced symbolist elements, such as the rainbow, the dove, and the owls.

Overleaf right: Eleanor Fortescue-Brickdale, 'The Introduction'. Deep in a wood, a young girl, again in medieval-looking dress, encounters three gnomes. The senior gnome is introducing one of his companions, who bows deeply, removing his hat. The scene is set in a brilliant Pre-Raphaelite style landscape and observed with remarkable fidelity.

LESSER FAIRY PAINTERS

Left: Etheline E. Dell, 'Titania's Bower'. *For a Victorian lady artist, Dell's work is quite surprisingly erotic. Her fairy pictures are entirely populated by beautiful naked fairies, lolling and sleeping in highly provocative attitudes. This Titania's Bower would seem calculated to appeal to the fantasies of Victorian male viewers.*

Right: Etheline E. Dell, 'Midsummer Fairies'. *Once again, Dell's vision of fairyland concentrates completely on female beauty. Lovely naked fairies sleep, disport and chatter among roses and other flowers by the light of a crescent moon. The scene is set within a proscenium arch, a device also used by Robert Huskisson.*

LESSER FAIRY PAINTERS

Left: Laura Gwenllian James, 'Where the Fairies dance in a place apart' (1905). *Laura James was the wife of Walter James, Lord Northbourne; both were extremely talented amateur artists. Her work is very rare, and a fairy subject such as this makes one wish she had painted more.*

Right: Sophie Anderson. 'Take the fair face of woman, and gently suspending With butterflies, flowers and jewels attending, Thus your fairy is made of most beautiful things'.
CHARLES EDE

Sophie Anderson was a painter of pretty and charming children, mostly girls. Only rarely did she depict them as fairies, as she has done here, giving the girl a head-dress of butterflies and butterfly wings. She holds an embroidered bag, presumably for her jewellery.

CHAPTER THIRTEEN

The Pre-Raphaelites and Fairies

John Everett Millais, 'Ferdinand lured by Ariel' (1849). *Millais' only attempt at a fairy subject, and one of the most remarkable of Pre-Raphaelite fairy pictures. The combination of medieval costume, brilliant colours, and the intensely green landscape setting, together with the ghostly figures of Ariel and her attendant goblins, give the picture a strange and hallucinatory atmosphere. Such a direct juxtaposition of reality and fantasy was clearly something Millais felt he could not repeat. The model for Ferdinand was Millais' fellow-artist and writer, F.G. Stephens.*

The Pre-Raphaelites' involvement with the fairy world was mainly through illustration. Paton's life-long friend Sir John Everett Millais (1829–96) only made one foray into fairyland with his *Ferdinand lured by Ariel*. This was one of his first great essays in the new Pre-Raphaelite style, and shows Ferdinand as a young man in medieval costume, listening as a ghostly green Ariel whispers in his ear. Ariel is surrounded by a circle of strange flying gnomes, and the action takes place in a brilliant Pre-Raphaelite landscape, one of the finest Millais painted. Here Millais is following the Pre-Raphaelite ideal of painting the landscape outdoors, in full sunlight, 'abjuring altogether brown foliage, smoky clouds, and dark corners', as Holman Hunt expressed it. The attempt to combine this with the ghostly apparition of Ariel and her attendants gives the picture the feeling of a hallucinatory dream. Trying to combine reality and fantasy in this way was neither possible nor successful, and may explain why Millais never painted such a picture again. But it is typical of the Pre-Raphaelites' determination to paint everything, from a blade of grass to the wrinkle of a medieval doublet and hose or the wings of a fairy, with total clarity. Thus fairies seem to become part of the real world. This is what gives Victorian fairy paintings their strangely disturbing edge. It is as if we are compelled to accept that the fairy world is part of the real world, not part of the subconscious or the imagination. Go for a walk in the English countryside, Millais seems to say, and you could meet Ariel and a flock of flying green

THE PRE-RAPHAELITES AND FAIRIES

Right: Henry Meynell Rheam, 'Once upon a Time'. *Rheam lived in Newlyn, and was friendly with many of the Newlyn School painters. He chose, however, to paint a completely different type of subject, focusing on allegorical and literary subjects.*

Below: Edward Burne-Jones, Frontispiece to 'The Fairy Family'. *Burne-Jones' first commission was to illustrate a book of European fairy tales entitled 'The Fairy Family'. It was never published in his lifetime, but the drawings survived, and were published in a modern edition in the 1980s.*

goblins, just as you might encounter a flock of birds. It is this attempt to depict the supernatural as if it was natural that makes Victorian fairy paintings so surreal.

Millais' picture *Ferdinand Lured by Ariel* is virtually the lone example of a fairy picture by a Pre-Raphaelite, and Millais did not repeat the experiment. William Bell Scott (1811–90), who was very much part of Pre-Raphaelite circles in spite of living and working in Newcastle-upon-Tyne, also ventured briefly into fairyland (pages 147 and 148); his painting *Cockcrow* of 1856 was based on 'A Fairy Tale' by Thomas Parnell.

Millais' life-long friend, Noel Paton, although not a member of the Pre-Raphaelite Brotherhood, made a far greater contribution to fairy painting with his two large *Oberon and Titania* paintings of the 1840s, and his superb *Fairy Raid* of 1867 (Chapter Nine). Apart from these, Paton only painted a few other fairy pictures, but his technique was the same as that used by Holman Hunt and Millais. He too painted with bright, pure colours, relentless attention to detail, and studied everything, where possible, directly from nature. Paton may not have known exactly what a fairy or goblin looked like, but he painted them so realistically as to make one believe that he did. This intensely bright and detailed technique was to influence most of the other fairy painters, such as John Simmons, John George Naish and John Anster Fitzgerald. So the Pre-Raphaelites were important for their influence on fairy painters, whose vision of fairyland was very much a Pre-Raphaelite one.

In 1855, Dante Gabriel Rossetti (1828–82), Millais and Arthur Hughes (1832–1915) were commissioned to illustrate William Allingham's collection of poems entitled 'The Music Master'. This contained his celebrated poem 'The Fairies', with its opening verse:

> Up the airy mountain
> Down the rushy glen
> We daren't go a'hunting
> For fear of little men;
> Wee folk, good folk,
> Trooping all together;
> Green jacket, red cap.
> And owl's white feather.

Rossetti and Millais contributed one plate each, Arthur Hughes seven; Rossetti's illustration was *The Maids of Elfen Mere* (page 37), which was seen by the young

THE PRE-RAPHAELITES AND FAIRIES

Burne-Jones and William Morris in Oxford, and fuelled both their admiration for the Pre-Raphaelites, and their desire to meet Rossetti. Burne-Jones (1833–98) was by this time working on his first illustrations for 'The Fairy Family'. This was never published in his lifetime, but all the illustrations for it survive. They reflect the influence of Dürer and early German engravers, but also of George Cruikshank, illustrator of 'Grimm's Fairy Tales'. In the later ones, the influence of Rossetti and the Pre-Raphaelites is also detectable. Thus Rossetti's *Maids of Elfen Mere* was an enormously important image, and influenced many subsequent illustrators, among them Frederick Sandys and Walter Crane. Arthur Hughes' illustrations for 'The Music Master' included a small, circular vignette of six trooping fairies. He also illustrated two of George MacDonald's 'Dealings with the Faeries' (1867) and 'At the Back of the North Wind' (1869).

Burne-Jones never became a fairy painter in the narrow sense of the word. When Rossetti agreed to take him on as a pupil, he declared that young Ned Jones was 'one of the nicest fellows in dreamland'. Burne-Jones' definition of a picture was 'a beautiful romantic dream', and dreamland was definitely his habitat. His great cycle of four pictures, *The Briar Rose,* is based on the story of 'The Sleeping Beauty'. and is a hymn to sleep and to dreams. Burne-Jones therefore deserves a place in any book on fairy painting, even though very few of his pictures can be called fairy pictures. He was one of the greatest Victorian dreamers and romantics, and thus the fairy world was very much part of his imagination. Fairy tales to him would have seemed just as real and just as relevant as the story of King Arthur and his knights. But when it came to painting, Burne-Jones was more likely to paint an angel than a fairy. 'The more materialistic science becomes', he declared defiantly, 'the more angels I shall paint'. Burne-Jones and the fairy painters could agree on one thing: the need to escape the horrors of the nineteenth century and fly away to the worlds of poetry, romance and the imagination.

Apart from *The Maids of Elfen Mere,* Rossetti's only other contribution to the fairy world were two illustrations for his sister Christina's poem 'Goblin Market (page 148). These show young girls tempted by the goblins' forbidden fruit and add to the suggestive atmosphere of the poem, which can be seen as a metaphor for sexual awakening. 'Goblin Market' was later illustrated by Laurence Housman. Rossetti produced no further fairy illustrations, but his influence on younger artists remained as potent as ever. Walter Crane, when a boy of twelve, saved up to buy the 1857 Moxon edition of Tennyson's poems which was illustrated by Rossetti, Millais and Holman Hunt. These illustrations had a great influence on Crane, who became and apprentice of W.J. Linton, a leading wood-engraver of the day. The 1860s was a brilliant decade for engraving and illustration, and many of the most talented younger artists began their careers as illustrators. Crane went on to become a famous illustrator of children's books. His work is part of that tendency towards prettification that effects all late Victorian fairy painting and

illustration. Crane's style also influenced a whole generation of later illustrators, such as Kate Greenaway and Margaret Tarrant.

Among the later Pre-Raphaelite painters, fairy subjects only occurred rarely. Most of them, like J.W. Waterhouse, preferred subjects from poetry, literature or Greek mythology. Later painters, such as Edward Reginald Frampton and Frank Cadogan Cowper, painted the usual range of aesthetic subjects, but only occasionally strayed into outright fantasy or fairy subjects. Two later Pre-Raphaelites who did were Henry Meynell Rheam and Edward Robert Hughes. Rheam (1859–1920), surprisingly lived in Newlyn, in Cornwall, but instead of

William Bell Scott, 'Ariel and Caliban'. *Bell Scott painted a few fairy subjects which display his marked taste for the grotesque. It was typical of him to choose the scene in 'The Tempest' where Ariel taunts Caliban and his friends:*

'At last I left them,/In the filthy mantled pool beyond your cell,/There dancing up to th' chins, that foul lake/O'erstunk their feet'.

THE PRE-RAPHAELITES AND FAIRIES

Right: Dante Gabriel Rossetti, 'Buy from us with a golden Curl'. *An illustration to the poem, 'Goblin Market' by Rossetti's sister, Christina, which describes sinister goblins who sell exotic fruit:*

One had a cat's face,
One whisked a tail,
One tramped at a rat's pace,
One crawled like a snail,
One like a wombat prowled
obtuse and furry;
One like a ratel tumbled hurry
skurry.

Far right: William Bell Scott, 'Hallow's Eve'. *The 1st November is All Hallows Saints' Day, and the evening before, Halloween, is traditionally a time for witches and spirits to make their appearance. Here a party of wee folk have raided a cellar, and are stealing beer from two large casks. Their revels have been interrupted by an astonished man, perhaps a publican, who has come down to the cellar with a candle, and a large flagon.*

painting fisherfolk, he remained faithful to romantic and literary subjects. His *Once upon a Time* (page 145) shows more of an affinity with princesses and goblins than with fairies, but these are very much part of the fairy world. Rheam's work is mainly in watercolour, and also shows an affinity with the work of Byam Shaw and Eleanor Fortescue-Brickdale.

Edward Robert Hughes is now mainly known for his fairy scene, *Midsummer Eve*, of circa 1908 (pages 134 and 135), but he did paint other fantasy subjects involving fairies and the spirit world. As we have seen, Hughes had impeccable

THE PRE-RAPHAELITES AND FAIRIES

Arthur Hughes, 'Jack o' Lantern' (1872). *In folklore Will'o the Wisp was a spirit who lived in bogs and marshes, and delighted in leading travellers astray. He was also known as Will o' the Wisp, Ingnus Fatuus, Spunkie, Walking Fire, Friar Rush and Fair Maid of Ireland. Hughes' main contribution to fairy painting was his illustrations for William Allingham's fairy poems, 'The Music Master'. This was the book also illustrated by Rossetti with 'The Maids of Elfen Mere' (1855).*

Pre-Raphaelite credentials; he was a nephew of Arthur Hughes and studio assistant to the ageing Holman Hunt, whom he helped with the large version of *The Light of the World* and the great *The Lady of Shalott*. Like Rheam, Byam Shaw and Fortescue-Brickdale, Hughes worked mainly in watercolour. His *Midsummer Eve*, although delightful, belongs firmly to the world of Peter Pan, rather than that of Victorian fairy painting. The fairy world depicted here is sweet and charming, but in no way mysterious or threatening to humans. This was the message of the Edwardian fairy picture.

Hughes could on occasion handle more sombre themes, as in his beautiful *Night with her Train of Stars* of 1912 (Birmingham City Art Gallery). This is an allegory of the death of a child, and shows an angel bearing aloft a baby, set against a night sky. This is not so much a fairy picture as a symbolist allegory.

Frank Cadogan Cowper, 'Titania Sleeps' (1928). *This extraordinary 1920s vision of an art deco Titania asleep in her glade shows how potent the appeal of fairy subjects could still be, well into the twentieth century. Cadogan Cowper (1877–1958) was positively the last of the Pre-Raphaelites, and went bravely on painting 'belles dames sans merci' until the 1950s.*

CHAPTER FOURTEEN

FAIRY ILLUSTRATORS 1850-1900

Kate Cameron, 'On the Rooftop'. *Kate Cameron was the sister of the Scottish painter David Young Cameron, and one of the few Glasgow School artists to turn to fairy subjects. Her work has a distinctly wistful charm, combined with a highly decorative manner typical of the Glasgow artists. She worked mainly in watercolour..*

From the beginning, nearly all fairy artists were involved in illustration. As we have seen, Dadd, Maclise, Huskisson, Fitzgerald, Cruikshank, and the Doyle brothers all worked as illustrators. So did Rossetti, Burne-Jones, Arthur Hughes, Crane and many of the Pre-Raphaelite followers. The purpose of this chapter is to explore some of the other Victorian artists involved in fairy illustration. Some were painters, for whom illustration was only a sideline, others were purely illustrators. The mid-Victorian period was a golden age for illustrators. New printing techniques, combined with a huge demand for illustrated papers, magazines and books meant that many of the most talented artists of the day turned to illustration. The most famous survey of the subject is Forrest Reid's 'Illustrators of the Sixties' (1928).

Many later illustrators were women, but only a few Victorian lady artists turned to fairy illustration. Two who did were Eleanor Vere Boyle and Kate Cameron. Eleanor Vere Boyle (1825–1916) was one of those distinguished lady amateurs whose work attained professional status, but she preferred to use only the initials EVB. Rather like the initials PRB, these were intended to be secret, and protect her anonymity, but of course most people in the art world knew who she was. Born Eleanor Vere Gordon, she married in 1845 the rector of Marston Bigot, in Somerset, the Hon. and Revd. Richard Boyle. Boyle was the younger son of the 8th Earl of Cork and rector on his father's estate at Marston, near Frome. Here Eleanor lived happily for forty years, combining her duties as rector's wife with a

FAIRY ILLUSTRATORS 1850–1900

remarkable career as an illustrator of children's books and using the money from her books to finance good works. She and her husband built a chapel, a well, and a splendid Gothic schoolhouse, now occupied by the author. Eleanor was also a painter, and designed stained glass windows. She was considered a great beauty when young and was painted by Sir William Boxall.

Most of EVB's books involved fairy stories. Her best-known is 'The Story without an End' which was published in 1879, with a beautiful cover stamped in black and gold of moths, ivy and spiders' webs. The fifteen colour plates were printed by the then new method of chromo-lithography, in bright, pure colours. Most of EVB's illustrations involve children with flowers, leaves and insects, and although the children are somewhat doll-like, the plates have a period charm. Much the same might be said of her other books, such as 'Child's Play' and 'Beauty and the Beast'. She also illustrated two versions of Hans Christian Andersen's 'Fairy Tales'. 'The Story without an End' by Sarah Austin is based on a German story by Carobé, and the style of EVB's illustrations is distinctly German, which

Above: Frederick George Cotman, 'Spellbound' (1912). *F.G. Cotman was the nephew of the great John Sell Cotman, and a member of a distinguished East Anglian artistic family. He painted a wide range of subjects, both in oil and watercolour; fairy subjects by him are a rarity.*

Left: Eleanor Vere Boyle, 'But He was only sunk in a Dream of Delight'. *An illustration from EVB's best-known book 'The Story without an End'. The brightly-coloured illustrations, with their doll-like and cherubic children, have a distinct German influence about them.*

FAIRY ILLUSTRATORS 1850–1900

Above: Annie French, 'The Butterfly'. *Like Kate Cameron, Annie French was a Glasgow artist with an exceptionally refined and delicate style. She combined pen, ink and watercolour with figures and landscape interwoven into elaborate art nouveau patterns.*

Right: Kate Cameron, 'Joy' (1892). *A winged fairy dances in the sunlight, playing with butterflies; the frame, too is decorated with butterflies.*

suggests that she may have studied the works of the Nazarenes and their followers. All EVB's children's books were published by Marston Low, and have now become collectors' items for those interested in nineteenth century illustrated books.

In 1886 Richard Boyle died, and Eleanor moved to Huntercombe Manor, near Burnham in Buckinghamshire. Here she devoted the rest of her life to gardening, and writing garden books, mostly illustrated with line drawings by herself. One of these, 'Days and Hours in a Garden', first published in 1884, became something of a best-seller, and was reprinted at least seven times.

Katherine Cameron (1874–1965), known as Kate, was the sister of the Scottish artist, David Young Cameron. She studied at the Glasgow School of Art, training ground of that remarkable group of artists known as the Glasgow Boys. These were the golden years of the Glasgow School. In the early 1900s, Kate began to illustrate children's books for the Edinburgh publishers T.C. & E.C. Jack. She

FAIRY ILLUSTRATORS 1850–1900

specialised in fairy stories and folk tales, for their series 'Told to the Children'. Her illustrations were done in watercolour, and are notable for their delicate charm, combining a wistful fantasy, with a soft and subtle range of colours. Like her brother, she was also a painter and etcher, and only regarded her illustration work as a sideline. Her work is in many ways typical of the Glasgow School and shows the influence not only of her brother, but also of other Glasgow artists such as Joseph Crawhall and Edwin Alexander. The Glasgow School produced a number of highly talented women artists and illustrators, among them Annie French (1872–1965), Jessie Marion King (1875–1949) and Phoebe Anna Traquair (1852–1936). Fairy princesses feature in all of their works, but they were none of them strictly speaking fairy artists. Romantic literary fantasy was more their line.

The same can be said of that most prolific of Victorian illustrators, Sir John Gilbert, RA (1817–97). He worked mainly in watercolour, continuing the romantic medieval tradition of George Cattermole. He illustrated nearly 150 books and produced nearly 30,000 illustrations for the 'Illustrated London News'. Most of his work was literary and historical, and he only occasionally produced a fairy subject. Gilbert was a typical Victorian success story: a Royal Academician, President of the Royal Watercolour Society, knighted in 1872, he died rich.

Another Victorian phenomenon was the immensely talented and prolific French artist, Gustave Doré (1832–83), whose large biblical pictures caused a sensation in England. He opened a gallery in Bond Street, known as the Doré Gallery, now Sotheby's saleroom. Like Gilbert, Doré was a prolific illustrator, and occasionally produced fairy and fantasy subjects. He is best known now for his extraordinary Dickensian illustrations of life in London's East End, for Blanchard Jerrold's book 'London – A Pilgrimage' (1872). Doré was nothing if not versatile, producing fairies one minute, and harrowing drawings of poverty the next. He also painted biblical epics, historical scenes, Scottish landscapes, birds and flowers. No wonder the Victorians thought him one of the marvels of the age.

More dedicated to illustration were two brothers, Charles Robinson (1870–1937), and the better-known William Heath Robinson (1872–1944). Both began their careers as illustrators for books and magazines, mainly in black and white. Charles' best known book was Robert Louis Stevenson's 'A Child's Garden of Verses' (1895). His brother William hoped to become a landscape painter, but found it easier to make a living as an illustrator. His first masterpiece was his set of outstanding illustrations for 'Rabelais' in 1904, revealing a talent for the grotesque equal to that of Rackham. He also illustrated a sumptuous edition of 'A Midsummer Night's Dream' in 1914, by then working in colour. During the First World War he began to work for humorous magazines, and it was as a comic illustrator that he was to make his name. During the 1920s and 1930s he became known as the 'Gadget King', producing drawings of weird yet utterly logical contraptions, gently mocking the inventions of the modern world. This is where

John Gilbert, 'The Enchanted Forest' (1885-6). *Gilbert was one of the most prolific of Victorian illustrators and watercolourists. He liked chivalric subjects involving Arthurian stories or episodes from English history. Here he has imagined two mounted knights in full armour, riding through a forest, where they are beset by a fantastical array of fairies who are endeavouring to tease and distract them as much as possible. A goblin has climbed up the lance of one of the knights. A rare example of chivalry and fairies combined.*

FAIRY ILLUSTRATORS 1850–1900

Above: Henry Justice Ford, 'The Princess carried off by the Bees'. *Ford was the illustrator of most of Andrew Lang's celebrated fairy books, which were hugely popular in children's nurseries at the turn of the century. This is an illustration from 'The Green Fairy Book' of 1911.*

his true genius lay, and the word 'Heath Robinson' has now entered the English language as a synonym for any improbable or fantastical gadget that is not likely to work, yet perversely does. Like all great illustrators, Robinson was able to imagine these strange machines as if they were totally real and entirely plausible. Like Rackham, he had the gift of conveying fantasy as if it was reality.

Andrew Lang's fairy books, beginning with 'The Blue Fairy Book' in 1889, were great favourites in late-Victorian and Edwardian nurseries. A new one came out almost every year, named after another colour, and they ended with 'The Lilac Fairy Book' in 1910. The main illustrator of all the books was Henry Justice Ford (1860–1914), a friend of Burne-Jones and, like him, a painter of historical and literary romantic subjects. But Ford's real talent was for illustration, both in pen and ink and in colour. Apart from Lang's Fairy Books, he illustrated 'Aesop's Fables' (1888) and 'The Arabian Night's Entertainment' (1898). In 1895 an exhibition of his watercolours, mostly from 'The Yellow Fairy Book', was held at the Fine Art Society in London. R.E.D. Sketchley, a noted writer on book illustration, wrote that Ford represented 'the modern art of fairy-tale illustration at its best,' and Gleeson White, who also wrote about illustrators, noted that he was 'a prime favourite with the small people'.

Although the late nineteenth century and early twentieth was a golden age of illustration, and of illustrated books, some of the greatest illustrators, such as Aubrey Beardsley and Laurence Housman, did not illustrate children's books, and did not therefore contribute to the fairy world. But many others did, especially after 1900, when the demand for children's books became a flood. Publishers discovered that there was a big demand for beautifully designed and illustrated children's books, especially at Christmas, and many artists turned to illustration after 1900. Of this new generation, the greatest illustrator, and the one to make the most impact on children's books and fairy stories, was Arthur Rackham.

Right: Charles Robinson, 'Each and all like ministering angels were, For the sensitive plant joy to bear'.

Charles Robinson was the brother of the better-known William Heath Robinson; both began their careers as book illustrators.

CHAPTER FIFTEEN

ARTHUR RACKHAM RWS
1867-1939

Arthur Rackham, 'Santa Claus' (1907). *Santa Claus trudges through the snow, attended by numerous goblins and dwarfs who help to carry his sacks of toys. They are all wearing traditional Father Christmas red hats with a white bobble. An illustration to 'Arthur Rackham's Book of Pictures' (1931).*

Golden the light on the locks of Myfanwy,
Golden the light on the book on her knee,
Finger-marked pages of Rackham's Hans
   Andersen
Time for the children to come down to tea.
JOHN BETJEMAN
'MYFANWY', 1940

With Rackham we come to the greatest of the turn-of-century illustrators, the man chosen by J.M. Barrie to illustrate 'Peter Pan', his most famous play, which opened in 1904. It was also to bring fame and fortune to Rackham.

Arthur Rackham was born in south London, the son of a civil servant. As a child he showed an aptitude for drawing, and in 1884 he entered Lambeth School of Art. His fellow-students included Charles Ricketts who was to remain both friend and mentor. To support himself Rackham worked in an insurance office from 1885 to 1892. Here he applied himself to work with the methodical accuracy and conscientiousness that were always to be characteristic of him. While working, he submitted drawings to papers and magazines, such as the 'Pall Mall Budget'. By 1892 he was ready to leave the insurance office, and joined the staff of the 'Westminster Budget'. Some of his early drawings, such as *The Influenza Fiend* of 1893, already show signs of his talent for the grotesque.

By the late 1890s, Rackham had embarked on his career as a book-illustrator, with 'The Ingoldsby Legends' (1898) and Charles and Mary Lamb's 'Tales from Shakespeare' (1899). These already show his style beginning to emerge. Like all

ARTHUR RACKHAM

Right: Arthur Rackham, 'The Fairies have their Tiff with the Birds' (1906). *Illustration from 'Peter Pan in Kensington Gardens', 1906, Rackham's lavish edition of Barrie's play. It is typical of his superb technique, combining pen and ink with a delicate colour range, and showing German and Japanese influences.*

Below: Pencil studies for a bookplate for Emma Williams Burlingham. *Rackham was an artist with a meticulous technique and a brilliantly incisive use of line. He presumably made studies like these for all his illustrations.*

great artists, Rackham managed to absorb many of the artistic currents of the 1890s and turn them into something of his own. Above all, he was a linear artist, a master of the 'bounding line' in pen and ink. In this respect, he saw himself as following Dürer and the early German printmakers. He also studied the work of many of his contemporaries, including George Cruikshank, Randolph Caldecott, Richard Doyle, and Arthur Boyd Houghton. He must have also been aware of the work of the Pre-Raphaelites and followers like Frederick Sandys and Walter Crane. By far the biggest influence on him, however, was the brilliant but short-lived Aubrey Beardsley, although Rackham also produced brilliant caricatures of Beardsley's style. The art nouveau influence of Beardsley and Charles Ricketts on Rackham is clearly detectable in his early work, especially the flowing lines of his cover and border designs. Gradually, this influence was to decline, as Rackham evolved his own uniquely personal style.

Another important influence on Rackham, especially on his colour plates, was the Japanese print. The delicacy of his flat areas of colour, combined with the fine, interlacing lines of his pen work, have a distinctly Japanese flavour and are reminiscent of the work of Hokusai. Most of Rackham's plates were printed in only three or four colours, which is why they have an almost monochrome appearance. In 1900, Rackham illustrated his first fairy book, 'Fairy Tales of the Brothers Grimm', for which he produced ninety-nine black and white drawings and a coloured frontispiece. This was an immediate success, and helped to establish his reputation as an illustrator of children's books. In 1903 he married Edyth Starkie, the daughter of an Irish Resident Magistrate, and herself a talented painter. Rackham had by this time exhibited his work at the Royal Academy, the Royal Watercolour Society, and elsewhere. In 1902 he became an Associate Member of the RWS and by 1908 a full member. He was also a member and chairman, of the Langham Sketching Club.

Rackham's reputation was further consolidated by his next book, 'Rip Van Winkle', published in 1905 with fifty-one colour plates. By this time the production of illustrated books was reaching a peak of lavishness and perfection

that has hardly been equalled since. The publisher usually produced a vellum and a cloth edition, as well as a de luxe vellum limited edition, signed and numbered by the author or illustrator. The publisher of 'Rip Van Winkle', William Heinemann, was to remain Rackham's publisher for many years. The original drawings were exhibited at the Leicester Galleries in the same year, where they nearly all sold. Among the illustrations were several of children and fairies, and others of bearded old men and dwarfs which clearly anticipate the films of Walt

Arthur Rackham, 'Peter Pan in the Fairies' Orchestra'. *The title page from 'Peter Pan in Kensington Gardens' (1906). Peter Pan as a child, sits on a toadstool playing the pan pipes, while fairies and elves whirl in dance.*

ARTHUR RACKHAM

Arthur Rackham, 'The Meeting of Oberon and Titania' (1908). *Rackham's version of the greatest of fairy scenes. A magnificent watercolour, it was one of the illustrations intended for Rackham's 'A Midsummer Night's Dream', but was not in the end used. This and the 'Peter Pan' illustrations were to influence many other Edwardian illustrators, among them Stephen Reid and Helen Jacobs.*

Disney. Thereafter, Rackham was to exhibit many of his illustrations at the Leicester Galleries, usually to coincide with the publication of a book.

It was the Leicester Galleries who arranged a meeting between Rackham and J.M. Barrie in June 1905. Barrie must have realised that he had found the perfect illustrator, and 'Peter Pan in Kensington Gardens' was published the following year. This contained many of Rackham's finest fairy illustrations, and the 'Pall Mall Gazette' commented: 'Mr Rackham seems to have dropped out of some cloud in Barrie's fairyland, sent by special providence to make pictures in tune to his whimsical genius'. As the title of the book implies, the story was set in Kensington Gardens – a deliberate combination of reality and fantasy. The settings, particularly the Serpentine Lake and Bridge, were immediately

Above: Arthur Rackham, 'Gerda is terrified by the Snow Queen's Advance Guard'. *Illustration to Hans Christian Andersen's 'The Snow Queen'.*

Right: 'Calling Shapes, and beckoning Shadows dire' (1914). *Illustration to an edition of Milton's 'Comus' (1921). Rackham's anthropomorphic trees, with their threatening and windblown posture, must have scared many young readers.*

recognisable to anyone familiar with the gardens, where George Frampton's famous statue of Peter Pan still stands. 'Peter Pan in Kensington Gardens' was to be the favourite Christmas book of 1906, and remained so for many years, going through several editions. Rackham's success led to the republication of several of his earlier books, often in more lavish editions, for which he made new illustrations. For the next twenty years, he was to remain the best known, and most highly paid English illustrator.

Rackham's later work is virtually a roll-call of fairy literature. There was hardly a book in the canon that he did not illustrate. He even lived long enough to illustrate Kenneth Grahame's 'Wind in the Willows', published in 1940 after Rackham's death, although the book itself had first been published in 1908, four

years after 'Peter Pan'. In 1906, Rackham's *annus mirabilis*, he also illustrated Kipling's 'Puck of Pook's Hill', which contained some fairy illustrations. The following year, 1907, saw his version of 'Alice's Adventures in Wonderland', and in 1908 followed 'A Midsummer Night's Dream', both key fairy sources. In 1909 came De La Motte Fouqué's 'Undine', the story so much admired by Burne-Jones and the Pre-Raphaelites. Rackham also illustrated several versions of Wagner's Ring Cycle.

Among Rackham's later books were 'Aesop's Fables' (1912), 'Mother Goose' (1913), 'A Christmas Carol' (1915), and Malory's 'Romance of King Arthur and his Knights of the Round Table', produced in 1917, at the height of the First World War. He also illustrated 'Cinderella' (1919), 'The Sleeping Beauty' (1920), James Stephen's 'Irish Fairy Tales' (1920), 'A Fairy Book' (1923), 'The Tempest' (1926), 'Goblin Market' (1933), 'The Pied Piper of Hamelin' (1934), as well as numerous other editions of Grimm and Hans Christian Andersen. In his life and work, Rackham virtually encapsulates the whole of Victorian fairy painting.

Rackham had many imitators, but none were able to equal the extraordinary precision of his style. Like all the greatest Victorian fairy artists, Rackham painted the denizens of fairyland as if he knew exactly what they looked like. Neither could Rackham's imitators capture the subtle strain of grotesque that runs through much of his work. They copied his delicacy, but the quality of his imagination eluded them. For although Rackham epitomises the Edwardian attitude to fairies, his work is never too sugary or sweet. His illustrations do at times have a genuine feeling of menace, particularly his gnarled old trees shaken by the wind. This is what sets him apart from the general run of Edwardian illustrators.

Although Rackham's work undoubtedly influenced Walt Disney, he never visited Hollywood, nor was he consulted directly. It is probably just as well, for he would not have liked the tendency towards prettification and trivialisation of the fairy world that Disney encouraged. Far better that Rackham's own uniquely imaginative vision should live on through his wonderful books, which have never been surpassed.

Above: Arthur Rackham, 'The Bird Woman and the Tree'. *Many of Rackham's illustrations show gnarled old trees which turn into gnarled old men. Here a tree-man converses with a bird.*

Left: Arthur Rackham, 'At last she met the Bridegroom who was coming slowly back'. *An illustration to Rackham's version of 'Grimm's Fairy Tales' published in 1917.*

CHAPTER SIXTEEN

FAIRY ILLUSTRATORS AFTER 1900

Kay Nielsen, 'This Good Fairy' (1912). *An illustration to 'Felicia' from 'In Powder and Crinoline' (1913) by Sir Arthur Quiller-Couch. Nielsen was one of the most stylish of the Edwardian illustrators, with a highly exotic style. In 1916 he returned to his native Denmark, to work for the Royal Danish Theatre. Later he worked in Hollywood for Walt Disney's 'Fantasia'.*

After 1900, the vogue for illustrated children's books, and especially Christmas gift books, became a craze. Publishers vied with each other to produce ever more lavish and beautiful editions, and this provided work for a whole new generation of illustrators. Many of the new illustrators were women; Beatrix Potter published her own first edition of 'The Tale of Peter Rabbit' in 1901. The tradition of talented women artists illustrating children's books continues to this day.

Not all the great illustrators of the Edwardian period worked on children's books. Many, such as Aubrey Beardsley, Sidney Herbert Sime, and Austin Osman Spare, were more interested in the worlds of history, literature and fantasy. As we have seen, Arthur Rackham was the greatest of the Edwardian fairy illustrators, and inevitably he had many rivals and imitators. The name most commonly grouped with his is that of Edmund Dulac (1882–1953). Dulac was born in Toulouse, and studied in Paris at the Académie Julian in 1904. A confirmed anglophile, he soon after moved to London, where he joined the London Sketch Club, and became a British subject. He made his name with an edition of the novels of the Brontë sisters (1905) for the publisher J.M. Dent. He then moved to Hodder & Stoughton, for whom he was to illustrate many books, beginning with 'Fairies I have met', by Mrs. Stawell (1910). He also illustrated lavish editions of 'Stories from Arabian Nights' (1907), 'The Tempest' (1908) and 'The Rubaiyat of Omar Khayyam' (1909). These early books show the influence of Rackham, but Dulac was already developing his own style, in

FAIRY ILLUSTRATORS AFTER 1900

Thomas Maybank, 'Come unto these yellow Sands' (1906). *Water sprites play and dance on the sea shore in this latter-day version of 'The Tempest', far removed in spirit from the earlier versions by Dadd and Huskisson. This is the fairy world softened and sweetened, and made acceptable to children.*

particular his use of a range of delicate blue-grey colours. Whereas Rackham was influenced by German engraving, Dulac was much more influenced by Oriental sources, especially Persian miniatures and Chinese art. Inevitably, he illustrated many of the same books as Rackham, such as 'The Sleeping Beauty' (1910) and 'Stories from Hans Andersen' (1911). In 1913 he illustrated another of Mrs. Stawell's books, 'My Days with the Fairies'. During the First World War, he became heavily involved with gift books, such as 'Princess Mary's Gift Book' (1914), 'King Albert's Book' (1914), and books by Queen Marie of Romania.

After the war, Dulac diversified considerably, becoming involved in portraits, the theatre, designing interiors, even composing music. He continued to illustrate a wide range of books, but only occasionally fairies. One of his last fairy books was 'A Fairy Garland' of 1928.

Another very stylish illustrator, whose career was similar to that of Dulac, was Kay Nielsen (1886–1957). Born in Copenhagen, he studied in Paris and came to London in 1911. Like Dulac he won a contract with Hodder & Stoughton, and illustrated for them 'In Powder and Crinoline' (1913) by Sir Arthur Quiller-Couch, and 'East of the Sun, West of the Moon' (1914). Nielsen evolved a highly ornamental, richly decorative style, compounded of Beardsley, Persian miniatures, and other exotic elements. He was also involved in theatrical design, and his work has similarities to both Charles Ricketts and Léon Bakst. Nielsen returned to Denmark in 1916, to work for the Royal Danish theatre. In the 1920s he moved to Hollywood and worked on Walt Disney's 'Fantasia', thus providing a palpable link between the world of fairy illustration and the cinema.

The demand for illustration attracted other foreign artists to London, such as the Hungarian-born William (Willy) Pogany (1882–1955). Pogany worked in Budapest and Paris before coming to London about 1905. He gained a considerable reputation as a book illustrator, chiefly due to his version of 'The Rubaiyat of Omar Khayyam' (1909). Pogany's style, like that of both Dulac and Nielsen, was exotic and highly ornamental, but did not often feature fairies. The decorative possibilities of fairy princesses was what interested these artists.

Another illustrator from Europe was the Viennese Georg Janny (1864–1935). He worked as a theatrical designer, and also painted allegorical and fantastical subjects, sometimes featuring fairies and other weird creatures. He died in Vienna.

William Pogany, 'Oh thou, who didst with pitfall and with gin Beset the road I was to wander in, Thou wilt not with predestination round enmesh me, And impute my fall to sin'.

Like Nielsen, Pogany came to England to work as an illustrator. His illustrations, though charming, contain hints of the macabre.

FAIRY ILLUSTRATORS AFTER 1900

Above: Honor C. Appleton, 'Then Katherine awoke'. *An illustration to 'The House of Fancy' by Mrs. H.C. Cradock (1922). Katherine has awoken to find her room full of elves and imps, who have even invaded her drawing board on the wall.*

Right: A. Duncan Carse, 'Bother the Gnat'. *Here a group of imps and elves are teasing a day-old chick. Unlike Fitzgerald, Carse sees the relationship between fairies and animals as whimsical and humorous. The cruelty and menace often present in Fitzgerald's work is entirely absent here.*

Among the myriad of Edwardian fairy illustrators, a few others are worthy of mention. William Henry Romaine Walker (1854–1940) managed to combine a career as an architect and interior designer with illustrating children's books. During the early 1900s he illustrated three books for John Lane, 'Tales of Jack and Jane', 'Nightcaps for the Babies', and 'Alice's Adventures in Wonderland'. Walker's illustrations are bright and colourful, but occasionally include fairy and fantasy subjects very much in the manner of Arthur Rackham. Walker came from a family of art dealers, and he held solo exhibitions of his watercolours at Walker's Galleries in the 1920s. By this time he seems to have given up illustration, to concentrate on his architectural work, which included designs for two extensions to the Tate Gallery for the Duveen family.

Also influenced by Rackham were Warwick Goble (1862–1948), Stephen Reid (1873–1948), Thomas Maybank (d. 1925) and A. Duncan Carse (d. 1938). Warwick Goble illustrated a number of fairy books, including 'The Water Babies' (1909), 'Green Willow and other Japanese Fairy Tales' by Grace James (1910), and Mrs. Craik's 'Fairy Book' (1914). Goble was also influenced by Oriental art, and like Dulac, combined this with his Rackhamesque style. He also illustrated books on Turkey for A. & C. Black, and worked both in pastel and watercolour. He exhibited his work regularly both at the Fine Art Society and Walker's Galleries. Stephen Reid was born in Aberdeen, and contributed illustrations to both books and magazines. Among his fairy illustrations were 'The Magic Casement' by Alfred Noyes (1908), and 'A Midsummer Night's Dream' (page 27). Thomas Maybank was both a painter and an illustrator, influenced by both Doyle and Rackham. He contributed fantastical fairy drawings to 'Punch' magazine, including 'A Bank Holiday in Goblin Land', 'The Coronation of Titania' and 'New Year's Eve'. He also illustrated Shakespeare's plays, and 'Nimphidia, the Court of Faerie' by Michael Drayton, a contemporary and friend of Shakespeare. Also in the Rackham orbit was A. Duncan Carse, a painter, muralist and illustrator who illustrated Hans Christian Andersen's 'Fairy Tales' and Lucy Scott's 'Dewdrops from Fairyland', both in 1912. Sydney Seymour Lucas (1888–1954) was the son of John Seymour Lucas, RA, and, like him, painted and illustrated historical subjects and occasional fairy and fantasy watercolours. He achieved great notoriety in

FAIRY ILLUSTRATORS AFTER 1900

Winifred Margaret Tarrant, 'A Fairy Band'. *Winifred Tarrant was the daughter of the illustrator, Percy Tarrant. She was a hugely prolific and popular illustrator of children's books. Like many illustrators, her work was widely disseminated by cards, prints, calendars and posters, published by the Medici Society, and is still popular today.*

1941 by publishing a scathing attack on modern art, which provoked heated correspondence in the 'East Anglian Daily Times'.

Women illustrators of fairies are also numerous after 1900. Many of them were influenced stylistically by the regency-style children of Kate Greenaway (1846–1901), a prolific and hugely successful illustrator of children's books, though not generally of fairies. The same could be said of two of Greenaway's imitators, Millicent Sowerby and Dorothy Wheeler. Millicent Sowerby (1879–1967) was the daughter of a Newcastle landscapist and botanical artist, John G. Sowerby. Dorothy Wheeler (1891–1966) also produced charming illustrations for children's books in the Greenaway manner and sweet style that generally prevailed after 1900.

Some of Greenaway's many followers developed distinctive styles of their own, notably Honor Appleton, Maud Tindal Atkinson, and Winifred Margaret

FAIRY ILLUSTRATORS AFTER 1900

Tarrant, all of whom did fairy subjects. Honor Appleton (1879–1951) trained as a painter, but after illustrating 'Bad Mrs. Ginger' in 1902, and Blake's 'Songs of Innocence' in 1910, she turned to professional illustration. Over the next thirty years, she was to illustrate over 150 books. Her soft and delicate style harks back to the Victorians, although she continued working in to the 1940s. Maud Tindal Atkinson (working 1906–37) produced illustrations for several nursery books for younger children, and these are therefore in a style deliberately more simplified and

Beatrice May Goldsmith, 'Do I like butter?' (1925). *Typical of the bright, cheerful and whimsical style that prevailed in children's books after 1900. The world of the fairies is now safely confined to the nursery.*

FAIRY ILLUSTRATORS AFTER 1900

Right: Helen Jacobs, 'Fairy watching a Girl Reading'. *This charming illustration sums up the transition of fairy painting into the world of children's books, a process that began with Doyle in the 1870s, and gathered pace after 1900. Helen Jacobs contributed to several Edwardian children's annuals, such as 'Little Folks', the title typical of the Edwardian attitude to fairies – something for the nursery, and no longer for the grown-ups*

Far right: Helen Jacobs, 'The Magic Mirror'. *Helen Jacobs produced her own, more feminine version of the Rackham style. She was the daughter of the writer W.W. Jacobs, evidence of the continuing connections between fairy painting and literature.*

child-like. Winifred Margaret Tarrant (1888–1959) was the daughter of an illustrator, Percy Tarrant. Her first book was an edition of Charles Kingsley's 'Water Babies' (1908), and thereafter she became a prolific and popular illustrator. Her bright and cheerful illustrations became widely known through the Medici Society, who published many of them in the form of cards, prints and calendars. Tarrant was a friend of Cecily Mary Barker (1895–1973) whose books of 'Flower Fairies' have

FAIRY ILLUSTRATORS AFTER 1900

Susan Beatrice Pearse, 'The Flyaway Horse'. *Susan Pearse (1878-1980) illustrated the 'Ameliaranne' series of books concerning girls and their dolls. She also contributed to the 'Children's Encyclopaedia' and to advertisements for Start-Rite Shoes. She was married to the portrait painter W.E. Webster.*

remained enormously popular to this day. Also influenced by Tarrant was Beatrice May Goldsmith (1895–1947) who trained as a painter and muralist, but also produced watercolours of children, mermaids and fairies.

Another highly influential figure was Mabel Lucie Attwell (1879–1964). Her rosy and doll-like pictures of children were a fixture in many a nursery and bathroom up to the 1940s and 1950s. Her work became widely known through cards, posters and calendars, also figurines and wall-plaques. By the 1920s she had become a household name. Although she did not do fairy subjects, her style influenced many illustrators who did. One was Anne Anderson (1874–1930) who was born in Scotland, later settled in England, and illustrated over 100 books, many with her illustrator husband, Alan Wright.

Helen Jacobs, RWS (1888-1970), the daughter of the writer W.W. Jacobs, became a well-known and prolific children's illustrator. She contributed to many annuals, among them 'Playbox', 'Rainbow' and 'Little Folks', and illustrated books for several leading publishers. Her style is a sweeter version of the Rackham manner, but without becoming too sugary.

Estella Canziani (1887-1964) was the daughter of an Italian engineer and an English portrait painter, Louisa Starr. Canziani lived all her life in Kensington Palace Green, near Kensington Palace in London, and gave her autobiography the title, 'Round about Three Palace Green' (1939). A talented writer, illustrator and artist, she is now largely remembered for one fairy subject, *The Piper of Dreams* (overleaf), shown at the Royal Academy in 1915. Prints of this became hugely popular, not only in nurseries but also, surprisingly, with soldiers in the trenches, many of whom wrote to the artist expressing their appreciation. Writing about her childhood, 'The Day of Reckoning' (1964), Mary Clive wrote that Canziani's prints 'hung over many a child's bed as a sort of honorary guardian angel'. Prints of *The Piper of Dreams* are still selling today; indeed it seems that fairies and the fairy world are as fascinating to the present generation as they were to our Victorian and Edwardian forebears.

FAIRY ILLUSTRATORS AFTER 1900

Above: Walter Jenks Morgan, 'Where rural Fays and Fairies dwell'. *Morgan (1847–1924) was a painter and illustrator from Birmingham; he worked as an illustrator for numerous magazines and book publishers. His occasional fairy pieces are full of that arcadian whimsy so typical at the turn of the century. Max Beerbohm remarked that Edwardian poetry was never short of fauns; nor was Edwardian painting.*

Right: Estella Canziani, 'Good Morning'. *A child finds a winged fairy hovering outside her window. Canziani signed her work with a star-shaped device, a reference to her mother, the painter Louisa Starr.*

Left: Estella Canziani, 'The Piper of Dreams' (1914). *Begun in the spring of 1914, when Canziani was staying with the classical scholar, Gilbert Murray. The model for the boy was the Murray's son Basil, and the background the woods behind their cottage. The watercolour was exhibited at the Royal Academy in 1915, in the midst of the First World War, and proved hugely popular. Over 250,000 prints of it were sold in the first year, many to soldiers in the trenches; perhaps fairyland helped them forget the horrors of war, although one wounded Tommy observed of Canziani's fairies, 'Don't you think she made them gnats rather large?'*

Above: A. Duncan Carse, 'Cats-Eye woos Moonstone'. *This brilliant watercolour shows the fantastical elegance and refinement of which Carse was capable. He evolved his own very individual brand of the Rackhamesque, turn-of-the-century style.*

Further Reading

Christian, John, *The Last Romantics,* exhibition catalogue, Barbican Art Gallery, London, 1989.
Guest, Ivor, *The Romantic Ballet in England: Its Derverlopment, Fulfilment and Decline,* 1954, repr. London, 1972.
Houfe, Simon, *Dictionary of 19th century British Book Illustrators and Caricaturists,* Woodbridge, 1978, 2nd edn., Woodbridge, 1996.
Maas, Jeremy, *Victorian Painters,* 1969; repr. London, 1988.
Maas, Jeremy, Gere, Charlotte, and others, *Victorian Fairy Painting,* exhibition catalogue with bibliography, Royal Academy, London, 1997–8.
Newall, Christopher, *Victorian Watercolours,* London, 1987.
Philpotts, Beatrice, *Fairy Paintings,* London, 1978.
Waterhouse, Ellis, *Dictionary of British 18th Century Painters,* Woodbridge, 1981.
Wood, Christopher, *The Dictionary of Victorian Painters,* 1971, 3rd edn., 2 vols., Woodbridge, 1995.
Wood, Christopher, *Victorian Painting,* London, 1999.

Monographs

'**Eleanor Vere Boyle**', Michael McGarvie, Frome Historical Research Group, Somerset, 1982.
'**Burne-Jones**', Christopher Wood, London, 1998.
'**Walter Crane,** Designer and Socialist', exhibition catalogue, Manchester City Art Gallery, 1989.
'**George Cruikshank**', exhibition catalogue, Victoria & Albert Museum (Arts Council), 1974.
'**The late Richard Dadd**', Patricia Allderidge, exhibition catalogue, Tate Gallery and elsewhere (Arts Council) 1974–5.
'**Francis Danby**' Francis Greenacre, exhibition catalogue, Tate Gallery and Bristol City Art Gallery, 1988.
'**Richard Doyle and his Family**', exhibition catalogue, Victoria & Albert Museum, 1983.
'**Edmund Dulac**', Colin White, London, 1976.
'**Daniel Maclise**', Richard Ormond, exhibition catalogue, National Portrait Gallery, London, and National Gallery of Ireland, Dublin, 1972.
'**Noel Paton**', M.H. Noel Paton and J.P. Campbell, Edinburgh, 1990.
'**Arthur Rackham**', Derek Hudson, London, 1960.
'**Arthur Rackham**', exhibition catalogue, Victoria & Albert Museum, 1979.

Plate List

Frontispiece: John Anster Fitzgerald, *The Fairies' Barque* (detail, see page 108)
Page 5: Ernest Howard Shepherd, *The Earth-Made House,* pen and ink, 10 x 19 cms. (4 x 7½ ins.). Chris Beetles Ltd., London
Page 8: John Anster Fitzgerald, *The Intruders* (detail, see page 10)
Page 9: John Simmons, *A Midsummer Night's Dream: Hermia and the Fairies,* signed and dated 1861, watercolour, 87 x 67 cms. (34½ x 26½ins.). Peter Nahum at the Leicester Galleries, London
Page 10: John Anster Fitzgerald, *The Intruders,* watercolour and bodycolour, 37 x 29 cms. (14½ x 11½ ins.). Photo Sotheby's
Page 11: Edmund Dulac, *E was an exquisite Elf,* 1906, signed and dated, pen, ink and watercolour, 24.1 x 19 cms. (9½ x 7½ ins.). Chris Beetles Ltd., London
Page 12: John Anster Fitzgerald, *In Fairyland,* watercolour and bodycolour, 34 x 47 cms. (13¼ x 18½ins.). Photo Sotheby's
Page 13: William Edward Frost, R.A., *Fairy Lovers,* pen, brown ink and watercolour, 17.8 x 11.4 cms. (7 x 4 ins). Chris Beetles Ltd., London
Page 14: Arthur Rackham, *The Daisy Fairy,* pen, ink and watercolour, 10.5 x 10.5 cms. (4 x 4 ins.). Chris Beetles Ltd., London
Page 15: *Frances and the Fairies,* photograph reproduced in 'The Coming of the Fairies' by Sir Arthur Conan Doyle, 1922
Page 15: Arthur Rackham, *Decorative Border with Fairies and Birds.* Chris Beetles Ltd., London
Page 16: Sir George Frampton, R.A., *Peter Pan,* signed, bronze. Fine Art Society, London
Page 17: John Anster Fitzgerald, *Ariel,* signed with monogram, watercolour and bodycolour, 47 x 29 cms. (18½ x 11½ ins.). Photo Sotheby's

Page 18: Johann Heinrich Fuseli, *Titania and Bottom* (detail, see pages 22–23)
Page 19: Circle of Francis Danby, *Fairies by a Rocky Stream,* oil on canvas, 34.2 x 27.3 cms. (13½ x 10¾ ins.). Peter Nahum at the Leicester Galleries, London
Page 20: William Blake, *Oberon, Titania and Puck with Fairies dancing,* c.1785, pencil and watercolour, 47.6 x 67.3 cms. (18¾ x 26½ ins.). Tate Gallery, London
Page 21: Francis Danby, *Scene from A Midsummer Night's Dream,* signed and dated 1832, watercolour, 19.7 x 27.9 cms. (7¾ x 11 ins.). Oldham Art Gallery, Lancashire
Pages 22–23: Johann Heinrich Fuseli, *Titania and Bottom,* c.1788–90, oil on canvas, 215.9 x 274.3 cms. (85 x 108 ins.). Tate Gallery, London
Page 24: John George Naish, *Titania* (detail, see page 26)
Page 25: Mary L. Gow, *Fairy Tales,* signed and dated 1880, oil on canvas, 46.2 x 36 cms. (18 x 14 ins.). Private Collection; photo courtesy Christopher Wood Gallery, London
Page 26: John George Naish, *Titania,* signed with monogram, oil on canvas, 35.6 cms. (14 ins.) diameter. Christopher Wood Gallery, London
Page 27: Stephen Reid, *A Midsummer Night's Dream,* signed and dated 1907, pen, black ink and watercolour, 22.8 x 33 cms (9 x 13 ins.). Private Collection
Page 29: John Anster Fitzgerald, *The Land of Nod,* watercolour and bodycolour, 25 x 35 cms. (9¾ x 13¾ ins.). Photo Sotheby's
Page 30: Circle of Joseph Noel Paton, *Dreams in Fairy Land,* oil on canvas, 24.8 x 34.3 cms. (9¾ X 13½ ins.). Peter Nahum at the Leicester Galleries, London

PLATE LIST

Page 33: Richard Doyle, *The God Thor drives the Dwarfs out of Scandinavia by throwing his hammer at them,* signed with monogram and dated 1878, watercolour, 48 x 67 cms. (19 x 26¼ ins.). Photo Sotheby's

Page 34: Sir John Tenniel, *A Fairy Piper,* signed with monogram, pastel on tinted paper, 23.5 x 12.7 cms. (9¼ x 5 ins.). Chris Beetles Ltd., London

Page 35: Sir Joseph Noel Paton, R.S.A., *Titania Asleep,* oil on canvas laid on card, 15.9 cms. (6¼ ins.) diameter. Peter Nahum at the Leicester Galleries, London

Page 36: George Cruikshank, Jnr., *A Fairy Dance,* pen, ink and watercolour, 26.8 x 42 cms. (10½ x 16½ ins.). Maas Gallery, London

Page 37: Dante Gabriel Rossetti, *The Maids of Elfen Mere,* woodcut illustration to William Allingham's poems 'The Music Master', 1855

Page 39: Adelaide Claxton, *Wonderland,* signed, watercolour heightened with white, 59.5 x 52 cms. (23½ x 20½ ins.). Christopher Wood Gallery, London

Page 41: Arthur Rackham, *The Introduction.* Chris Beetles Ltd., London

Page 42: John Anster Fitzgerald, *A Midsummer Night's Dream* (detail, see pages 44–45)

Page 43: Charles Rolt, *Prospero relating his history to Miranda,* oil on canvas, 36.8 x 28.6 cms. (14½ x 11¼ ins.). Forbes Magazine Collection, New York © All rights reserved

Pages 44–45: John Anster Fitzgerald, *Titania and Bottom, a scene from A Midsummer Night's Dream,* signed, also signed, inscribed and titled on reverse, oil on canvas, 44.4 x 68.6 cms. (17½ x 27 ins.). French and Co., New York

Page 46: Daniel Maclise, R.A., *Priscilla Horton as Ariel,* 1838–9, oil on panel, 67.5 x 54.5 cms. (26½ x 21½ ins.). The R.S.C. Collection, by permission of the Governors of the Royal Shakespeare Theatre

Page 49: George Cruikshank, *Queen Mab,* oil on canvas, 48.3 x 50.8 cms. (19 x 20 ins.) diameter. Forbes Magazine Collection, New York © All rights reserved

Page 50: John Anster Fitzgerald, *The Birds' Nest,* signed with initials FG, watercolour and bodycolour, shaped top, 25.3 x 19 cms (10 x 7½ ins.). Christopher Wood Gallery, London

Page 51: Edward Henry Corbould, *A Fairy Scene, Rothkappchen,* signed and dated 1855, watercolour, 36.5 x 53 cms. (14½ x 20¾ins.). The Royal Collection © Her Majesty The Queen

Page 52: Richard Doyle, *The Attar Cup in Aagerup – the Moment of Departure* (detail, see page 56)

Page 53: Edmund Thomas Parris, *The Visit at Moonlight,* signed and dated 1832, oil on canvas, 35.5 x 50.8 cms. (14 x 20 ins). Maas Gallery, London

Page 54: Circle of Richard Doyle, *The Dance of the Pixies,* oil on board, 10.2 x 31.8 cms. (4 x 12 ins.). Maas Gallery, London

Page 55: Alfred Edward Chalon, R.A., *La Sylphide: Souvenir d'Adieu,* signed with initials AEC, RA, and dated 1845, watercolour heightened with white, numbered 4 from a series of 6, 40.6 x 27.9 cms. (16 x 11 ins.). Private Collection

Page 56: Richard Doyle, *The Attar Cup in Aagerup – the Moment of Departure,* signed with initials, watercolour, 25.5 x 46 cms. (10 x 18 ins.). Photo Sotheby's

Pages 56–57: Robert Alexander Hillingford, *The Fairy Dance,* inscribed on label on reverse, oil on canvas, in a painted oval, 40 x 53 cms. (15¾ x 20¾ ins.). Christopher Wood Gallery, London

Page 58: Arthur Rackham, *A Fairy Song* (detail, see page 61)

Page 59: Follower of Sir Joseph Noel Paton, *Fairy Music,* or *Bonny Kilmeny;* inscribed with titles on reverse, oil on board, 37.5 cms. (14¼ ins.) diameter. Photo Sotheby's

Page 60: John Anster Fitzgerald, *Fairy Musicians,* signed with initials FG, watercolour and bodycolour, shaped top, 25.3 x 19 cms. (10 x 7½ ins.). Christopher Wood Gallery, London.

Page 61. Arthur Rackham, *A Fairy Song,* 1930, signed, pen, ink and watercolour, 33.6 x 27.3 cms. (13¼ x 10¾ ins.). Chris Beetles Ltd., London.

Page 62: Daniel Maclise, *Undine* (detail, see page 64)

Page 63: Theodore von Holst, *Fairy Lovers,* c.1840, oil on canvas, 41.3 x 31.1 cms. (16¼ x 12¼ ins.). Tate Gallery, London.

Page 64: Daniel Maclise, R.A., *Undine,* 1844, oil on panel, 44.4 x 60 cms. (17¼ x 23½ ins.). The Royal Collection © Her Majesty the Queen

Page 65. James Elliot, *Fairies playing in a Birds' Nest,* watercolour and bodycolour, 19 x 24.8 cms. (7½ x 9¾ ins.). Chris Beetles Ltd., London

Pages 66–67: Sir Edwin Landseer, R.A., *Scene from A Midsummer Night's Dream, Titania and Bottom,* 1848–51, oil on canvas, 82 x 133 cms. (32¼ x 52¼ ins.). National Gallery of Victoria, Melbourne.

Page 68: James Eliot, *Fairies and Fruit,* signed with monogram, watercolour and bodycolour, 17.8 x 33 cms. (7 x 13 ins.). Chris Beetles Ltd., London

Page 69: David Scott, R.S.A., *Puck fleeing before the Dawn,* signed and dated 1837, oil on canvas, 95.3 x 146 cms. (37½ x 57½ ins.). National Gallery of Scotland, Edinburgh

Pages 70–71: Robert Huskisson, *The Midsummer Night's Fairies – There sleeps Titania,* 1847, oil on panel, 29.8 x 35.5 cms. (11¾ x 14 ins.). Forbes Magazine Collection, New York © All rights reserved

Page 72: Robert Huskisson, *Come unto these Yellow Sands,* 1847, oil on panel, 34.9 x 45.7 cms. (13¾ x 18 ins.). Private Collection

Pages 74–75: Richard Dadd, *The Fairy Feller's Master Stroke,* 1855–64, signed and inscribed on reverse, oil on canvas, 54 x 39.4 cms. (21¼ x 15½ ins.). Tate Gallery, London

Page 77: Richard Dadd, *Come unto these Yellow Sands',* signed and dated 1842, oil on canvas, 55.3 x 77.5 cms. (21½ x 31 ins.). Photo Sotheby's

Pages 78–79: Richard Dadd, *Titania Sleeping,* c.1841, oil on canvas, 64.8 x 77.5 cms. (25½ x 30½ ins.). Musée du Louvre, Paris

Page 80: Richard Dadd, *The Haunt of the Fairies,* c.1841, oil on canvas, oval, 56 x 47.3 cms. (22 x 18½ ins.). Forbes Magazine Collection, New York © All rights reserved

Page 82. Photograph of Richard Dadd at work on *Contradiction: Oberon and Titania,* c.1856. Bethlem Royal Hospital Archives and Museum

Page 83: Richard Dadd, *Contradiction: Oberon and Titania,* 1854–8, oil on canvas, oval, 61 x 75.5 cms. (24 x 29¾ ins.). Collection Lord Lloyd-Webber

Pages 84–85: Richard Dadd, *Contradiction: Oberon and Titania* (3 details, see page 83)

Page 86: Sir Joseph Noel Paton, R.S.A., *The Quarrel of Oberon and Titania* (detail, see page 90)

Page 87: Sir Joseph Noel Paton, R.S.A., *Puck and the Fairy,* signed with monogram, oil on card, 24.2 x 28 cms. (9½ x 11 ins.). Chris Beetles Ltd., London.

Pages 88–89: Sir Joseph Noel Paton, R.S.A., *The Reconciliation of Oberon and Titania,* signed and dated 1847, oil on canvas, 76.2 x 122.6 cms. (30 x 48¼ ins.). National Gallery of Scotland, Edinburgh

Pages 90–91: Sir Joseph Noel Paton, R.S.A., *The Quarrel of Oberon and Titania,* 1849, oil on canvas, 99 x 152 cms. (38 x 60 ins.). National Gallery of Scotland, Edinburgh

Page 92: After Sir Joseph Noel Paton, R.S.A, *The Pursuit of Pleasure,* 1855, engraving. Maas Gallery, London

Page 93: Sir Joseph Noel Paton, R.S.A., *The Fairy Raid* (2 details, see pages 94–95)

Pages 94–95: Sir Joseph Noel Paton, R.S.A., *The Fairy Raid: Carrying off a Changeling, Midsummer Eve,* 1867, oil on canvas, 90.5 x 146.7 cms. (35½ x 57¾ ins.). Glasgow Museums: Art Gallery and Museum, Kelvingrove

Pages 96–97: Sir Joseph Noel Paton, R.S.A., *Under the Sea I and II,* both signed with monogram, oil on panels, 33 cms. (13 ins.) diameter. Photos Sotheby's

PLATE LIST

Page 98: John Anster Fitzgerald, *Robin defending his Nest* (detail, see page 103)

Page 99: John Anster Fitzgerald, *The Artist's Dream*, signed and dated 1857, oil on board, 25.4 x 30.5 cms. (10 x 12 ins.). Maas Gallery, London

Page 100: John Anster Fitzgerald, *Fairies attacking a Bat*, watercolour and bodycolour, 35.5 x 54 cms. (14 x 21¼ ins.). Photo Sotheby's

Page 101: John Anster Fitzgerald, *The Pond Fairies*, signed, watercolour and bodycolour on buff paper, 28 x 43 cms. (11 x 17 ins.). Photo Sotheby's

Page 102: John Anster Fitzgerald, *The Enchanted Forest*, signed and inscribed on an old label on reverse, watercolour and bodycolour, 48 x 71 cms. (19 x 28 ins.). Photo Sotheby's

Page 103: John Anster Fitzgerald, *Robin defending his Nest*, c.1858–60, oil on canvas, oval, 30.5 x 40.6 cms. (12 x 16 ins.). Photo Sotheby's

Page 104: John Anster Fitzgerald, *The Captive Dreamer*, 1856, oil on board, 26 x 31.5 cms. (10¼ x 13¼ ins.). Peter Nahum Ltd., London

Page 105: John Anster Fitzgerald, *The Stuff that Dreams are made of*, c.1858, signed, oil on board, 25.4 x 30.5 cms. (10 x 12 ins.). Private Collection; photo courtesy Maas Gallery, London

Page 106: John Anster Fitzgerald, *The Fledgling*, watercolour, arched top, 26.5 x 43 cms. (10¼ x 16¾ ins.). Maas Gallery, London

Page 107: John Anster Fitzgerald, *The Fairies' Banquet*, signed and dated 1859, oil on canvas, 24.8 x 29.7 cms. (9¾ x 11¾ ins.). Private Collection

Page 108: John Anster Fitzgerald, *The Fairies' Barque*, 1860, oil on canvas, 26 x 31.1 cms. (10¼ x 12¼ ins.). Private Collection

Page 109: John Anster Fitzgerald, *Who killed Cock Robin?*, oil on canvas, oval, 29.2 x 39.3 cms. (11½ x 15½ ins.). Photo Maas Gallery, London

Page 110: John Anster Fitzgerald, *The Fairy's Funeral*, 1864, oil on canvas, 24.8 x 29.7 cms. (9¾ x 11¾ ins.). Private Collection

Page 111: John Anster Fitzgerald, *The Fairy Falconer*, signed with initials FG, watercolour, 17.8 x 20.3 cms. (7 x 8 ins.). Christopher Wood Gallery, London

Page 112: Joseph Oppenheim, *Old J.A. Fitzgerald*, signed with initials and dated 1903, and inscribed below mount, pencil, 17.2 x 12.1 cms. (6¾ x 4¾ ins.). Chris Beetles Ltd., London

Page 112: John Anster Fitzgerald, *The Old Hall, Fairies by Moonlight*, signed, watercolour, 21.5 x 24 cms. (8½ x 9½ ins.). Peter Nahum at the Leicester Galleries, London

Page 113: John Anster Fitzgerald, *Christmas Eve*, signed, watercolour and bodycolour, 30 x 44.5 cms. (12 x 17½ ins.). Peter Nahum at the Leicester Galleries, London.

Page 114: Richard Doyle, *The Triumphal March of the Elf King* (detail, see page 117)

Page 115: Richard Doyle, *Temptation*, signed with monogram, watercolour and bodycolour, 13 x 11 cms. (5¼ x 4¼ ins.). Photo Sotheby's

Page 116: Richard Doyle, *An Intruder*, *Reposing*, and *Fairy Child's Play*, 3 plates from 'In Fairyland' by William Allingham, 1869–70. Peter Nahum Ltd., London

Page 117: Richard Doyle, *The Triumphal March of the Elf King* and *Courtship Cut Short*, 2 plates from 'In Fairyland'. Peter Nahum Ltd., London

Page 118: Richard Doyle, *The Tournament* and *Rehearsal in Elfland – musical Elf teaching the young Birds to sing*, 2 plates from 'In Fairyland'. Peter Nahum Ltd., London

Page 119: Richard Doyle, *The Fairy Queen takes an airy Drive*, and *Teasing a Butterfly*, 2 plates from 'In Fairyland'. Peter Nahum Ltd., London

Page 120: Charles Altamont Doyle, *Hearts are Trumps*, watercolour, 25.5 x 36.9 cms. (10 x 14½ ins.). Peter Nahum at the Leicester Galleries, London

Page 121: Charles Altamont Doyle, *A Dance around the Moon*, pen, ink and watercolour, 24.8 x 38.7 cms. (9¾ x 15¼ ins.). Maas Gallery, London

Page 122: Charles Altamont Doyle, *The Fairy Queen, a Procession*, signed and dated 1882, pen, ink and watercolour, 21.6 x 52.7 cms. (8½ x 20¾ ins.). Maas Gallery, London

Page 122: Charles Altamont Doyle, *The Dragon Chariot*, pen, ink and watercolour, 15.5 x 50.5 cms. (6 x 20 ins.). Peter Nahum at the Leicester Galleries, London

Page 123: Charles Altamont Doyle, *The Fairy Picnic*, signed and dated Oct.1882, watercolour, 23 x 40 cms. (9 x 15¾ ins.). Peter Nahum at the Leicester Galleries, London

Page 124: John George Naish, *Moon Fairies I* (detail, see also page 126)

Page 125: John George Naish, *Elves and Fairies: A Midsummer Night's Dream*, 1856, oil on panel, 35.6 x 45.7 cms. (14 x 18 ins.). Photo Sotheby's, New York

Page 126: John George Naish, *Moon Fairies II*, signed and dated 1853, oil on panel, 28 x 38 cms. (11 x 15 ins.). Photo Sotheby's

Page 127: John Simmons, *The Honey Bee Steals from the Bumble Bees*, signed, watercolour and bodycolour, oval, 26.7 x 21 cms. (10½ x 8¼ ins.). Photo Maas Gallery, London.

Page 128: John Simmons, *A Fairy among Convolvulus*, watercolour and bodycolour, oval, 26.5 x 21 cms. (10½ x 8¼ ins.). Peter Nahum Ltd., London.

Page 129: John Simmons, *The Evening Star*, signed, watercolour and bodycolour, 29 x 38 cms. (11½ x 15 ins.). Peter Nahum at the Leicester Galleries, London

Page 130: Thomas Heatherley, *Fairy seated on a Mushroom*, c.1860, oil on canvas, 29.8 x 24.1 cms. (11¾ x 9½ ins.). Private Collection; photo courtesy Maas Gallery, London

Page 131: Thomas Heatherley, *Fairies among Mushrooms*, c.1860, oil on canvas, 19.7 x 27 cms. (7¾ x 10⅝ ins.). Maas Gallery, London

Page 132: Atkinson Grimshaw, *Iris, Spirit of the Rainbow*, 1876, signed, oil on canvas, 70 x 90 cms. (27½ x 35½ ins.). Peter Nahum at the Leicester Galleries, London

Page 133: Edward Robert Hughes, *Midsummer Eve*, watercolour and bodycolour, signed, 114.3 x 76.2 cms. (45 x 30 ins.). Private Collection; photo courtesy Sotheby's

Pages 134–135: Edward Robert Hughes, *Twilight Fantasies*, signed, watercolour and bodycolour, 73.7 x 108 cms. (29 x 42½ ins.). Private Collection; photo courtesy Maas Gallery, London

Page 136: Eleanor Fortescue-Brickdale, *The Lover's World*, 1905, signed on a scroll, watercolour and bodycolour, 111.8 x 66 cms. (44 x 26 ins.). Bristol Museums and Art Gallery.

Page 137: Eleanor Fortescue-Brickdale, *The Introduction*, signed with monogram on a scroll, pencil and watercolour, 48.8 x 32.2 cms. (19 x 12½ ins.). Private Collection; photo courtesy Christopher Wood Gallery, London

Page 138: Etheline E. Dell, *Titania's Bower*, signed, titled on label on reverse, oil on panel, 35.5 x 30 cms. (14 x 12 ins.). Photo Sotheby's

Page 139: Etheline E. Dell, *Midsummer Fairies*, signed and inscribed with title, watercolour and bodycolour, 19.7 x 16.2 cms. (7⅝ x 6⅜ ins.). Maas Gallery, London

Page 140: Laura Gwenllian Jones, *Where the Fairies dance in a place apart*, signed and dated 1905, also inscribed with title on reverse, oil on panel, 29.8 x 22.8 cms. (11¾ x 9 ins.). Private Collection; photo courtesy Christopher Wood Gallery, London

Page 141: Sophie Anderson, *Take the fair face of woman*, oil on canvas, 52.7 x 41.3 cms. (20¾ x 16¼ ins.). Exhibited Royal Society of British Artists 1869 no. 239. Maas Gallery, London

Page 142: William Bell Scott, *Hallow's Eve* (detail, see page 149)

Page 143: Sir John Everett Millais, Bt., P.R.A., *Ferdinand lured by Ariel*, signed and dated 1849, oil on panel, arched top, 64.8 x 50.8 cms. (25½ x 20 ins.). The Makins Collection/Bridgeman Art Gallery

Page 144: Edward Burne-Jones, Frontispiece to *The Fairy Family*, taken from an album, all pen and ink, each page 30.5 x 30.5 cms. (12 x 12 ins.). Photo Sotheby's.

Page 145: Henry Meynell Rheam, *Once upon a Time*, signed, watercolour and bodycolour, 78.5 x 43 cms. (31 x 17 ins.). Private Collection; photo courtesy Christopher Wood Gallery, London

PLATE LIST

Page 147: William Bell Scott, *Ariel and Caliban*, signed, and signed and inscribed on reverse, 61 x 77.5 cms. (24 x 30½ ins.). Peter Nahum at the Leicester Galleries, London

Page 148: Dante Gabriel Rossetti, *Buy from us with a golden Curl*, print taken from 'Goblin Market' by Christina Rossetti

Page 149: William Bell Scott, *Hallow's Eve*, signed and inscribed on a label on reverse, oil on canvas, 78 x 56 cms. (30¾ x 22 ins.). Exhibited Royal Scottish Academy 1848 no. 327. Photo Sotheby's

Page 150: Arthur Hughes, *Jack o'Lantern*, signed and dated '72, inscribed on a label on reverse, oil on canvas, 48.3 x 73.7 cms. (19 x 29 ins.). Peter Nahum at the Leicester Galleries, London

Page 151: Frank Cadogan Cowper, *Titania Sleeps*, signed and dated 1928, oil on canvas, 91.4 x 114.3 cms. (36 x 45 ins.). Private Collection; photo courtesy Christopher Wood Gallery, London

Page 152: Sir John Gilbert, R.A., *The Enchanted Forest* (detail, see page 158)

Page 153: Katherine Cameron, *On the Rooftop*, signed, watercolour, 28 x 19.2 cms. (11 x 7¾ ins.). Chris Beetles Ltd., London

Page 154: Eleanor Vere Boyle, *But He was only sunk in a Dream of Delight'*, coloured plate from 'The Story without an End' by Sarah Austin, 1879. Author's Collection

Page 155: Frederick George Cotman, *Spellbound*, signed and dated 1912, also signed and inscribed on backboard, watercolour, 54 x 76 cms. (21¼ x 29⅞ ins.). Private Collection; photo courtesy Christopher Wood Gallery, London

Page 156: Annie French, *The Butterfly*, signed twice, once with initials, pen, ink and watercolour, 14 x 22.2 cms. (5½ x 8¾ ins.). Chris Beetles Ltd., London

Page 157: Katherine Cameron, *Joy*, signed and dated 1892, watercolour, 53.3 x 35.6 cms. (21 x 14 ins.). Chris Beetles Ltd., London

Page 158: Sir John Gilbert, R.A., *The Enchanted Forest*, signed with monogram and dated 1885–6, watercolour, 111.8 x 127 cms. (44 x 50 ins.). Guildhall Art Gallery, Corporation of London/Bridgeman Art Library

Page 160: Henry Justice Ford, *The Princess carried off by the Bees*, print taken from 'The Green Fairy Book' by Andrew Lang, 1911

Page 161: Charles Robinson, *Each and all like ministering angels were*, signed with initials, watercolour, 17.2 x 8.9 cms. (6¾ x 3½ ins.). Chris Beetles Ltd., London

Page 162: Arthur Rackham, *Calling Shapes, and beckoning Shadows dire*, (detail, see page 169)

Page 163: Arthur Rackham, *Santa Claus*, 1907, pen, ink and watercolour, 36.8 x 28.6 cms. (14½ x 11¼ ins.). Chris Beetles Ltd, London

Page 164: Arthur Rackham, *Pencil studies for a bookplate for Emma Williams Burlingham*, inscribed, pen, ink and pencil, 27.3 x 19 ins (10¾ x 7½ ins.). Chris Beetles Ltd., London

Page 165: Arthur Rackham, *The Fairies have their Tiff with the Birds*, signed and dated 1906, pen. ink and watercolour, 24.7 x 27.3 cms. (9¾ x 10¾ ins.). Chris Beetles Ltd., London

Page 166: Arthur Rackham, *Peter Pan in the Fairies' Orchestra*, signed and dated '06, pen, ink and watercolour. Chris Beetles Ltd., London

Page 167: Arthur Rackham, *The Meeting of Oberon and Titania*, signed and dated '05, pen, ink and watercolour, 21.5 x 34.3 cms. (8½ x 13½ ins.). Chris Beetles Ltd., London

Page 168: Arthur Rackham, *Gerda is terrified by the Snow Queen's Advance Guard, but she said 'Our Father' and is rescued by Little Bright Angels*, signed, pen, ink and watercolour, 19 x 28.1 cms. (7½ x 11 ins.). Chris Beetles Ltd., London

Page 169: Arthur Rackham, *Calling Shapes, and beckoning Shadows dire*, signed and dated 1914, pen, ink and watercolour, 30.5 x 24.8 cms. (12 x 9¾ ins.). Chris Beetles Ltd., London

Page 170: Arthur Rackham, *At last she met the Bridegroom who was coming slowly back*, signed, pen, ink and watercolour, 36.2 x 26 cms (14¼ x 10¼ ins.). Chris Beetles Ltd., London

Page 171: Arthur Rackham, *The Bird Woman and the Tree*, signed with initials, black chalk and watercolour, 22.8 x 13.3 cms. (9 x 5¼ ins.). Chris Beetles Ltd., London.

Page 172: A. Duncan Carse, *Bother the Gnat* (detail, see page 177)

Page 173: Kay Nielsen, *This Good Fairy*, illustration from 'In Powder and Crinoline'. Photo Victoria and Albert Museum, London/Bridgeman Library, London

Page 174: Thomas Maybank, *Come unto these yellow Sands*, signed and dated 1906, oil on canvas, 51 x 74 cms. (20 x 29 ins.). Peter Nahum at the Leicester Galleries, London

Page 175: William Pogany, *Oh thou. who did'st with pitfall and with gin*, signed, watercolour and bodycolour, 29.8 x 20.3 cms. (11¾ x 8 ins.). Chris Beetles Ltd., London.

Page 176: Honor C. Appleton, *Then Katherine awoke*, signed and inscribed with title, pencil, watercolour and bodycolour, 26.8 x 19 cms. (10½ x 7½ ins.). Chris Beetles Ltd., London

Page 177: A. Duncan Carse, *Bother the Gnat*, signed, pen, ink and watercolour, 30.5 x 20.3 cms. (12 x 8 ins.). Chris Beetles Ltd., London

Page 178: Winifred Margaret Tarrant, *A Fairy Band*, signed, pen, ink and watercolour, 49.2 x 61.8 cms. (19¾ x 24¼ ins.). Collection Averil and Barry Miles

Page 179: Beatrice May Goldsmith, *Do I like Butter?*, 1925, signed and inscribed with title on reverse, watercolour over pencil, 34.9 x 27.9 cms. (13¾ x 11 ins.). Chris Beetles Ltd., London

Page 180: Helen Jacobs, *Fairy watching a Girl reading*, signed, pen, ink, watercolour and bodycolour, 36.2 x 25.4 cms. (14¼ x 10 ins.). Chris Beetles Ltd., London

Page 181: Helen Jacobs, *The Magic Mirror*, signed, pen, ink, watercolour and bodycolour, 24.2 x 20.3 cms. (9½ x 8 ins.). Chris Beetles Ltd., London

Page 182: Susan Beatrice Pearse, *The Flyaway Horse*, watercolour, size not known. Chris Beetles Ltd., London

Page 183: Walter Jenks Morgan, *Where rural Fays and Fairies dwell*, signed, watercolour, 19 x 45.1 cms. (7¾ x 17¾ ins.). Exhibited Royal Academy 1900 no. 1180. Maas Gallery, London

Page 183: Estella Louisa Michaela Canziani, *Good Morning*, signed with monogram, watercolour and bodycolour, 27.9 x 19 cms. (11 x 7½ ins.). Chris Beetles Ltd., London

Page 184: Estella Louisa Michaela Canziani, *The Piper of Dreams*, signed with monogram C in a star, watercolour and bodycolour, 46.9 x 34.2 cms. (18½ x 13½ ins.). Photo Maas Gallery, London

Page 185: A. Duncan Carse, *Cats-Eye woos Moonstone*, signed, watercolour, 25.3 x 38.1 cms. (10 x 15 ins.). Chris Beetles Ltd., London

Page 192: John Anster Fitzgerald, *Titania and Bottom, a scene from A Midsummer Night's Dream* in a reconstructed twiggy frame (details on pages 44-45).

Index

Page numbers in bold indicate an illustration

'Aesop's Fables', 160, 171
Albert, Prince, 51, 64, 66
'Alice's Adventures in Wonderland', 8, 34, 38, 91, 171, 176
Allingham, William, 37, 116, 144, 150
'Ameliaranne' books, 182
Andersen, Hans Christian, 12, 32, 35, 38, 40, 48, 155, 168, 171, 174, 176,
Anderson, Anne, 182
Anderson, Sophie, 131, 140, **141**
Appleton, Honor C., 178–180, **176**
'Arabian Nights, The', 32, 38, 160, 172
architecture, 8
'Art Journal', 73,
'Art Union', 73, 74, 76
Art Worker's Guild, The, 48
Arthur, King, 146, 159
'Arthur Rackham's Book of Pictures', **163**
Ashbee, C.R., 48
'At the Back of the North Wind', 146
Atkinson, Maud Tindal, 178–179
Attwell, Mabel Lucie, 38, 182
Austin, Sarah, 155

Bakst, Léon, 175
Ballantyne, John, 93
ballet and dance, 11, 13–14, 36, 42, 47, 48, 52–57, 58, 62, 66, 77, 102–103, 112
Barker, Cecily Mary, 38, 180, 182
Barrie, Sir J(ames) M(atthew), 40, 41, 42, 51, 162, 164, 167
Barry, Sir Charles, 81
Beardsley, Aubrey, 160, 164, 172, 175
'Beauty and the Beast', 38, 155
Berlioz, Hector, 58
Bethlem Royal Hospital, 74, 81, 82
Blake, William, 11, 18, 20, 84, 110, 179, **20**
'Book of British Ballads', 34, 76
Bosch, Hieronymus, 85, 103
Boydell, Alderman John, 18, 20
Boydell's Gallery, 20
Boyle, Eleanor Vere, 38, 152, 155–156, **155**
Boyle, Richard, Hon. and Revd., 152, 155, 156
Briar Rose, The, 32, 144
British Institution, 100, 108, 111, 124
Broadmoor, 81, 85
Brown, Ford Madox, 85
Brown, John, 60

Brueghel, Pieter, 103
Burne-Jones, Sir Edward, 15, 32, 33, 37, 126, 129, 132, 144, 146, 152, 160, 171, **144**

Caldecott, Randolph, 164
Cameron, David Young, 152, 156
Cameron, Katherine (Kate), 152, 156, 159, **152, 157**
'Canterbury Tales, The', 24
Canziani, Estella, 16, 182, 183, 185, **183, 184**
Carobé, 155
Carolsfeld, Schnorr von, 66
Carr, J. Comyns, 48
Carroll, Lewis, 34, 38, 91
Carse, A. Duncan, 176, **177, 185**
Celtic literature and folklore, 15, 24, 34–35, 36–37, 38, 65, 86, 91–93, 171
Chalon, Alfred Edward, 52–53, **54, 55**
Chaucer, Geoffrey, 12, 18, 24
'Children's Encyclopaedia', 182
'Child's Garden of Verses, A', 159
'Christmas Carol, A', 171
'Cinderella', 171
Claxton, Adelaide, 38, 130–131, **39**
Claxton, Florence, 130
Clique, The, 74
Coleridge, Samuel Taylor, 34
'Coming of the Fairies, The', 14, 41
Conan Doyle, see Doyle Sir Arthur
Corbould, Edward Henry, 34, 76, 51
'Coronation of Titiania, The', 176
Cotman, Frederick George, 131, 155
Cotman, John Sell, 131, 155
Cottingley fairies, 14, 40–41, 121, **15**
Cowper, Frank Cadogan, 34, 147, 151, **151**
Crane, Walter, 37, 38, 48, 126, 146–147, 152, 164
Croker, Thomas Crofton, 35, 65, 110
Crowquill, Alfred, 34, 76
Cruikshank, George, 12, 35, 37, 40, 84, 146, 152, 164, **49**
Cruikshank, George Jnr., **36**

Dadd, Richard, 13, 16, 34, 48, 70, 73, 74–85, 86, 88, 93, 106, 117, 120, 122, 126, 152, 174, 176, **75, 77–80, 82, 83**
Dalziel Brothers, 117
'Damnation of Faust, The', 58
Danby, Francis, 16, 62, **19, 21**
Danish mythology, 32, 56
'Day and Night Songs', 37,

'Days and Hours in a Garden', 156
'Dealings with Faeries', 146
Dell, Etheline, E., 130, 138, 139, **138, 139**
Diaghilev, Sergei, 54
Dickens, Charles, 8, 12, 35–36, 48, 66, 84
Dicksee, Frank, 34
Disney, Walt, 40, 41, 51, 166–167, 171, 172, 175
Dodgson, Rev. C.L., see Carroll Lewis
Doré, Gustave, 159
Doyle, Sir Arthur Conan, 14, 41, 121, 123
Doyle, Charles Altamont, 120–123, 152, **120–123**
Doyle, John, 114
Doyle, Richard 'Dickie', 16, 32, 37, 84, 114–119, 120, 126, 152, 164, 176, 180, **33, 54, 56, 115–119**
Drury Lane theatre, 70
Dulac, Edmund, 16, 40, 172, 174–175, 176, **11**
Dürer, Albrecht, 40, 146, 164

Eliot, George, 34
Elliott, James, 64, 68, **65, 68**
Etty, William, 13, 26, 42, 70, 73, 88–89
EVB, see Boyle, Eleanor Vere

'Faerie Queene, The', 26, 38, 60
'Fairy Family, The', 37, 144, 146, **144**
'Fairy Legends...of the South of Ireland', 35, 65
'Fairy Mythology, The', 34, 56
Fairyland Lustre, 38
'Falstaff', 58
'Fantasia', 40, 172, 175
'Faust', 62
Fitzgerald, John Anster, 11, 12, 13, 16, 29, 45, 93, 98–113, 114, 117, 126, 144, 152, 176, **frontispiece, 10, 12, 17, 29, 44, 45, 50, 60, 99, 100–113**
Fitzgerald, William, 98, 100
folklore, 12, 15–16, 18, 32, 34–35, 56, 64, 65, 86, 91–93, 107, 109, 110, 111, 130, 147
Folklore Society, 15, 34
Ford, Henry Justice, 38, 160, **160**
Fortescue-Brickdale, Eleanor, 130, 134, 148, 150, **136, 137**
Fouqué, Baron De La Motte, 66, 171
Frampton, Edward Reginald, 147
Frampton, Sir George, 168, **16**
Frazier, J.G., 34
French, Annie, 156, 159, **156**

French literature, 24, 26, 32
Frith, William Powell, 47, 70, 73, 74, 81
Frost, William Edward, 13, 26, 42, 70, 73, 88–89, **13**
Fuseli, Johann Heinrich, 11, 18, 20–21, 62, 65, 68, 120, **22, 23**

Gautier, Théophile, 52, 53
German literature and mythology, 24, 32, 66, 155, 171
Gilbert, Sir John, 34, 76, 159, **158**
Gilbert, Sir William S., 58, 60
'Giselle', 53
Glasgow School, 156, 159
Goble, Warwick, 176
'Goblin Market', 37, 146, 171, **148**
Goethe, 62, 68
'Golden Bough, The', 34
Goldsmith, Beatrice May, 182, **179**
Gow, Andrew Carrick, 24
Gow, Mary L., 24, **25**
Grahame, Kenneth, 40, 168
Greenaway, Kate, 38, 147, 178
Grimm Brothers, 12, 32, 34, 35, 40
'Grimm's Fairy Tales', 12, 34, 35, 38, 146, 164, 171, **170**
Grimshaw, John Atkinson, 16, 126, 128–129, **132**
Grosvenor Gallery, 60, 119

Hall, Samuel Carter, 34, 7, 76
Hardy, Thomas, 15
Haydon, Benjamin Robert, 31–32
Heatherley, Thomas, 126, **130, 131**
Herrick, Robert, 32, 107
Hillingford, Robert Alexander, 56, **56, 57**
Hodson, Geoffrey, 41
Hollywood, 40, 41, 171, 172, 175
Holst, Theodore von, 67, 68, **63**
Hood, Dr. William Charles, 81, 83, 84
Horton, Miss Priscilla, 31, 47, 66, **46**
Houghton, Arthur Boyd, 164
Housman, Laurence, 146, 160
Howard, Henry, 21
Hughes, Arthur, 37, 126, 129, 132, 144, 146, 150, 152, **150**
Hughes, Edward Robert, 16, 129–130, 132, 134, 147, 148, 150, **133, 134, 135**
Hunt, William Henry 'Birds' Nest', 64, 68, 103, 108–109
Hunt, William Holman, 38, 114, 129, 132, 142, 144, 146, 150
Huskisson, Robert, 13, 16, 34, 48, 70–73, 76, 77, 86, 88, 93, 98, 124, 139, 152, 174, **71, 72**

'Illustrated London News, The', 100, 101, 159

INDEX

'In Fairyland, or Pictures from the Elf World', 37, 116, **116–119**
'In Powder and Crinoline', 172, 175, **175**
'Ingoldsby Legends, The', 162
'Iolanthe', 60
'Irish Fairy Tales', 171

Jacobs, Helen, 167, 180, 182, **181**
Jacobs, W.W., 180, 182
James, Laura Gwenllian, 131, 140, **140**
James, Walter, Lord Northbourne, 131, 140
Janny, Georg, 175
Jonson, Ben, 32

Kean, Charles, 14, 28, 31, 42, 47–48, 112
Keats, John, 34
Keightley, Thomas, 34, 35, 56, 110
Kelmscott Press, 38
Kemble, Charles, 112
'King of the Golden River, The', 116
King, Jessie Marion, 40, 159
Kingsley, Charles, 37, 180
Kipling, Rudyard, 40, 171

'L'Allegro', 32
'La Belle Dame Sans Merci', 34
'La Sylphide', 13, 52, 54, 102
'Lady of the Lake, The', 34, 35, 92
Lamb, Charles and Mary, 162
Lamb, John, 62
Landseer, Sir Edwin, 16, 47, 66, 67, **67**
Lang, Andrew, 38, 160
Lang's Fairy Books, 38, 159–160
'Lay of the Last Minstrel, The', 34
literature, 8, 11, 15, 18, 24–41, 147, 168, 172, 180
'Little Folks', 180, 182
Lucas, Sydney Seymour, 176, 178

MacBeth, Robert Walker, 118
MacDonald, George, 38, 39, 146
Maclise, Daniel, 15, 16, 31, 35, 47, 62, 65–66, 74, 76, 86, 88, 93, 98, 106, 117, 152, **46, 64**
Macready, William Charles, 31, 42, 47, 70, 112
'Maids of Elfen Mere, The', 37, 144, 146, 150, **37**
Makeig-Jones, Daisy, 38
Malory, Sir Thomas, 171
Martin, John, 21
masques, 48
Maybank, Thomas, 176, **174**
Medici Society, 178, 180
Mendelssohn, Felix, 58
Meredith, George, 34
'Midsummer Night's Dream, A', 12, 13 14, 20, 24, 26, 27–30, 42, 47, 48, 52, 58, 62, 65, 66, 67, 68, 69, 70, 74, 76, 81–82, 83, 87,

Midsummer Night's Dream continued
88–91, 98, 124, 130, 138, 139, 159, 171, 176, **8, 20–23, 26, 27, 44, 45, 67, 69, 70, 78, 79, 87, 89, 167**
Millais, Sir John Everett, 13, 16, 37, 38, 76, 86, 142, 144, 146, **143**
Milton, John, 12, 21, 32, 168
'Minstrelsy of the Scottish Border', 34, 92
Morgan, Walter Jenks, 183, **183**
Morris, William, 32, 33–34, 37, 38, 144, 146
'Mother Goose', 32, 171
Murray, Basil, 185, **184**
music and opera, 11, 42, 48, 52, 54, 58–61, 117, 118, 175
'Music Master, The', 37, 146, 150
Mussorgsky, 40
mythology, see folklore

Naish, John George, 26, 124, 144, **26, 125, 126**
Nazarene painters, 66, 156
Nielsen, Kay, 40, 172, 175, **173**
Noel Paton, see Paton
Nordic mythology, 32, 33–34,
North, John William, 118
Northbourne, Lord, see James
'Nutcracker Suite, The', 54

'Oberon's Feast', 32, 107
'Ondine', 53, 66
O'Neil, m H.N., 74
Oppenheim, Joseph, **112**

pantomime, 32, 41, 42, 47, 48, 54, 101, 102
'Paradise Lost', 21, 32
Parris, Edmund Thomas, 62, **53**
'Patience', 60
Paton, Sir Joseph Noel, 13, 15, 16, 34, 35, 38, 47, 48, 76, 86–97, 98, 106, 117, 124, 144, **30, 35, 59, 87, 89, 90, 94–97**
Paxton, Joseph, 108
Pearse, Susan Beatrice, 182, **182**
Perrault, Charles, 32
Perrot, Jules, 53, 66
Peter Pan, 168, **16**
'Peter Pan, or the Boy who wouldn't grow up', 8, 16, 51, 60, 130, 162, 171
'Peter Pan in Kensington Gardens', 40, 41, 164, 167, 168, **165, 166**
photography, 14, 40–41
Pinwell, George John, 118
poetry, 11, 34, 146, 147, 183
Pogany, William (Willy), 175, **175**
Pope, Alexander, 32
Potter, Beatrix, 172
Pre-Raphaelites, 8, 11, 34, 38, 67, 86, 88, 89, 91, 118, 124, 130, 134, 142–151, 152, 164, 171
Primus, see Lamb, John

'Princess and the Goblin, The', 38
'Princess Mary's Gift Book', 174
'Puck of Pook's Hill', 40, 171
'Punch', 34, 114, 116, 176

Quiller-Couch, Sir Arthur, 171, 175

'Rabelais', 159
Rackham, Arthur, 16, 40, 159, 160, 162–171, 172, 174, 176, 180, 182, 185, **14, 15, 41, 61, 163–171**
Reid, Stephen, 167, 176, **26**
Reynolds, Sir Joshua, 18, 20, 21
Rheam, Henry Meynell, 144, 147–148, 150, **145**
Ricketts, Charles, 162, 164
'Rip van Winkle', 40, 164, 166
Roberts, David, 81
Robinson, Charles, 40, 159, 161, **161**
Robinson, William Heath, 40, 159–160, 161
Rolt, Charles, 42, **43**
'Romeo and Juliet', 48, 58, 66
'Rose and the Ring, The', 36, 62
Rossetti, Christina, 37, 146
Rossetti, Dante Gabriel, 37, 126, 144, 146, 150, **37**
Royal Academy, 16, 66, 68, 73, 76, 100, 114, 119, 159, 164, 182, 185
Royal Academy Schools, 74, 86
Royal Institute of Oil Painters, 130
Royal Scottish Academy, 86, 91, 120
Royal Society of British Artists, 68, 100
Royal Watercolour Society, 159, 164
'Rubaiyat of Omar Khayyam, The', 172, 175
'Rusalka', 60
Ruskin, John, 11, 36, 38, 66, 116

Sainthill, Mr., 62, 65
Sambourne, Linley, 38
Sandys, Frederick, 37, 146, 164
Schwind, Moritz von, 66
Scott, David, 67–68, 69, **69**
Scott, Sir Walter, 32, 34–35, 68, 92
Scott, William Bell, 34, 67, 144, **149**
Shakespeare, William, 12, 13, 18, 20, 24, 26, 27, 29, 31, 42, 47, 52, 58, 66, 68, 92, 162, 176
Shaw, Byam, 130, 148, 150
Shelley, Percy Bysshe, 34
Shepard, Ernest Howard, **5**
Siddal, Elizabeth, 105
Simmons, John, 8, 124, 126, 131, 144, **127, 128**
'Sleeping Beauty, the', 171, 174
'Snowman, The', 38, 48
Society for Psychical Research, 14
'Songs of Innocence', 179

Sowerby, Millicent, 178
Spenser, Edmund, 12, 26, 38, 60
spiritualism, 14, 40–41, 132
Starr, Louisa, 182, 183
Start-Rite Shoes, 182
Stevenson, Robert Louis, 159
'Stolen Child, The', 38
'Story without an End, The', 38, 155
Sugar Plum Fairy, 54
Sullivan, Sir Arthur, 58, 60
'Symphonie Fantastique', 58

Taglioni, Madame Marie, 13, 52–53, 54, **55**
'Tales from Shakespeare', 162
Tarrant, Percy, 178, 180
Tarrant, Winifred Margaret, 38, 147, 178–179, 180, 182, **178**
Tchaikovsky, Piotr, 54
'Tempest, The', 12, 14, 27, 30–31, 47–48, 52, 58, 62, 68, 69, 70, 73, 76–77, 98, 114, 143, 171, 172, **43, 46, 72, 77, 143**
Tenniel, Sir John, 34, 38, 70, **34**
Tennyson, Alfred, Lord, 146
Terry, Ellen, 29, 47
Terry, Kate, 48
Thackeray, William Makepeace, 36, 62, 116
theatre, 11, 14, 42–51, 70–73, 101, 139, 175
'Through the Looking Glass', 34, 38
Thumb, General Tom, 31–32
Traquair, Phoebe Anna, 159
Tree, Herbert Beerbohm, 48
Turner, J.M.W., 16, 66

'Undine, 32, 171

Verdi, Giuseppe, 58
Vestris, Elizabeth, 47
Victoria, Queen, 35, 51, 60, 62, 64, 66, 98

Wagner, Richard, 34, 58, 60, 171
Walker, Fred, 118
Walker, William Henry Romaine, 176
'Walpurgis Night's Dream, A', 62
Ward, Edward Matthew, 47,
'Water Babies, The', 37–38, 176, 180
Waterhouse, John William, 34, 147
Weber, Carl, 58
Webster, W.E., 182
Wedgwood Fairyland Lustre, 38
Wheeler, Dorothy, 178
Wilson, Henry, 48
'Wind in the Willows, The', 40, 168
Wright, Alan, 182
Wyatt, Benjamin, 70

Yeats, William Butler, 38